granny square crochet

granny square crochet

35 contemporary projects using traditional techniques

Catherine Hirst

CICO BOOKS

LONDON NEW YORK

Published in 2012 by CICO Books
An imprint of
Ryland Peters & Small Ltd
20–21 Jockey's Fields
London WC1R 4BW

www.cicobooks.com

10 9 8 7 6 5 4 3 2 1

A CIP catalogue record for this book is
available from the British Library.

ISBN 978 1 908170 88 0

Printed in China

Managing editor: Gillian Haslam
Editor: Marie Clayton
Pattern checker: Susan Horan
Designer: Roger Hammond
Photographer: Emma Mitchell
Stylist: Sophie Martell

For digital editions, visit
www.cicobooks.com/apps.php

contents

introduction

The humble granny square gets a modern reinterpretation in 35 projects ranging from accessories through to home goods and items for baby. I love the ingenious construction of a granny square, which lends itself so well to creative application in a variety of patterns. Granny squares are also in fashion right now, with garments and accessories made from these traditional squares appearing everywhere from couture catwalks to high street shops.

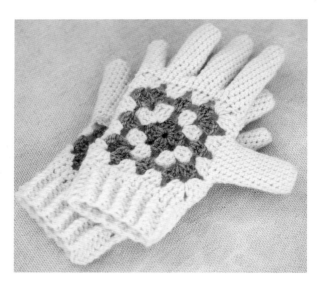

The astute reader will notice some projects are not, in fact, made of squares. The brilliant granny stripe stitch pattern takes the 3-treble grouping basis of granny squares and converts it into a lively striped pattern that works up quickly and easily, providing style and versatility. In other projects, the granny square construction is applied to create shapes other than squares, such as hexagons and triangles.

One great technique you will see used often in these pages is the join-as-you-go technique, described in detail on page 121. I recommend you get to grips with this technique, because it's not difficult once you've mastered it and it means no more joining stacks and stacks of squares. Instead, you join each square to the previous one in the last round of working, which means that when you've finished all the squares, you've finished the piece. What a relief!

Special attention is paid to the edging in these projects; the sides of granny squares – and especially granny stripes – can sometimes look unfinished, so many items have an edging added to make them look complete and professional. The edgings used – such as crab stitch, shell stitch and popcorn stitch – will become invaluable tools in your crocheted projects once you see how finished and attractive your work looks with a lovely edge incorporated.

Many of the projects, such as the baby blankets, tea cosy and cushion covers, can be modified to fit the size and shape you need; instructions on how to adapt

for a custom fit are given. I encourage you to modify the patterns to suit – choose colours that work with your décor, the shapes that are most attractive to you, and resize if necessary to fit to perfection! Feel free to use a different weight of yarn than that suggested on projects where tension is not important, but be aware that this will make a different-size final piece: thicker yarns and a larger hook will make

a larger item, whereas thinner yarn and a smaller hook will make a smaller one.

The projects made from individual squares or other repeating shapes lend themselves beautifully to reinterpretation. Love the flower square in the pram blanket? Why not make a strip of them, add one of the many edgings contained within these pages, and create a gorgeous scarf in your favourite colours? Or take the granny hexagon from the table runner, add an extra strip or two of hexagons for more width, and make yourself a glamorous evening wrap? Let your imagination run wild!

Possibly the best thing about the majority of these projects is that they are wonderful stash-busting exercises. Whatever yarn you happen to have lurking in a drawer or basket or on a shelf can be used up – even very small amounts – to make colourful and beautiful items, so all that yarn you have left over from other projects won't go to waste. There is very little yarn out there that wouldn't work for these projects – although I would suggest sticking with cotton yarn for the flannels on page 32 and acrylic or other machine-washable synthetic for the dog coat on page 55. However, if you do choose to use the yarns suggested you'll find that most of it is economically priced.

Each project has a skill level listed, so crocheters new to the craft can start with the easy projects and work their way up to the more advanced, such as the cosy Granny Square Gloves on page 72 and the gorgeous Teddy Bear on page 102. For a starter project I would suggest the Granny Square Cushion Cover on page 34, since it's a beautiful item that will teach you all you need to know about granny square construction. A note for left-handed crocheters: additional information is

given in patterns when the left-handed crocheter will need to work a certain section in a specific way. As a leftie myself, I know how hard it can be to interpret a pattern when no notations are added for the southpaws!

It's time for the granny square to say goodbye to its humble, old-fashioned origins and take its rightful place as a crochet technique for the modern world. You'll be surprised how easily and quickly most of these projects work up. I had tremendous fun creating these pieces, and I hope you will too. My sincerest thanks to you, the reader, for buying this book!

chapter 1

for the home

Adorn and warm your home with beautiful, granny-inspired
items, from the ever-popular tea cosy to exciting new
interpretations of cushion covers, place mats and
table runners. These projects would also
work brilliantly as housewarming
or wedding gifts!

granny round cushion cover

A little bit retro, a little bit modern… This fast and easy cushion cover combines the best of both! The front is made in granny rounds, while the back is in striped rounds. A shell edging adds a feminine touch. You can use colours to match your décor and make a whole collection of these charming cushion covers.

Skill level: Easy

Materials

100% merino wool chunky (bulky) weight yarn, such as Wendy Merino Chunky

* 1 x 50g ball (approx 65m/71yd) each in deep pink (A), pale grey (B), blue-green (C)
* 2 x 50g balls (approx 130m/142yd) in lilac (D)
* 6.0mm (US size J/10) crochet hook
* 40cm (16in) diameter cushion pad

Dimensions

* Cushion is 40cm (16in) in diameter. Rounds can be added or subtracted to customize for your own cushion.
* Exact tension is not important on this project.

Front

Using A, ch5, join with ss in first ch to form a ring.

Rnd 1: Ch3, 15tr in ring, join with ss in top of first ch-3.
Fasten off A.

Rnd 2: Attach B in any st, ch3, 2tr in same st as join, *ch1, miss 1 st, 3tr in next st; rep from * to end of rnd, ch1, miss last st, join with ss in top of first ch-3 (8 sets of 3 tr made).
Fasten off B.

Rnd 3: Attach C in any ch-1 sp, ch3, [2tr, ch1, 3tr] all in same sp as join, [3tr, ch1, 3tr] in each sp around, join with ss in top of first ch-3.
Fasten off C.

Rnd 4: Attach D in any ch-1 sp, ch3, 2tr in same sp as join, ch1, [3tr, ch1] in each ch-sp and each sp between 3-tr sets around, join with ss in top of first ch-3.
Fasten off D.

Rnd 5: Attach A in any ch-1 sp, ch3, 2tr in same sp as join, *[3tr, ch1, 3tr] in next ch-1 sp, 3tr in next ch-1 sp; rep from * to end, [3tr, ch1, 3tr] in last ch-1 sp, join with ss in top of first ch-3.
Fasten off A.

Rnd 6: Using B instead of D, work as Rnd 4.

Rnd 7: Attach C in any ch-1 sp, ch3, 2tr in same sp as join, *[3tr, ch1, 3tr] in next ch-1 sp, 3tr in each of next two ch-1 sps; rep from * to end, [3tr, ch1, 3tr] in next ch-1 sp, 3tr in last ch-1 sp, join with ss in top of first ch-3.

Rnds 8–10: Rep Rnd 4, changing colours as set each rnd.
Fasten off.

Back

Using A, ch5, join with ss in first ch to form a ring.

Rnd 1: Ch3, 11tr in ring, join with ss in top of first ch-3.
Fasten off A.

Rnd 2: Attach B in any st, ch3, 1tr in same st as join, 2tr in each st around, join with ss in top of first ch-3. (24 sts)
Fasten off B.

Rnd 3: Attach C in any st, ch3, 1tr in same st as join, [1tr in next st, 2tr in next st] around, 1tr in last st, join with ss in top of first ch-3. (36 sts)
Fasten off C.

Rnd 4: Attach D in any st, ch3, 1tr in same st as join, [1tr in each of next 2 sts, 2tr in next st] around, 1tr in each of last 2 sts, join with ss in top of first ch-3. (48 sts)
Fasten off D.

Rnd 5: Attach A in any st, ch3, 1tr in same st as join, [1tr in each of next 3 sts, 2tr in next st] around, 1tr in each of last 3 sts, join with ss in top of first ch-3. (60 sts)
Fasten off A.

Rnd 6: Attach B in any st, ch3, 1tr in same st as join, [1tr in each of next 4 sts, 2tr in next st] around, 1tr in each of last 4 sts, join with ss in top of first ch-3. (72 sts)
Fasten off B.

Rnd 7: Attach C in any st, ch3, 1tr in same st as join, [1tr in each of next 5 sts, 2tr in next st] around, 1tr in each of last 5 sts, join with ss in top of first ch-3. (84 sts)
Fasten off C.

Rnd 8: Attach D in any st, ch3, 1tr in same st as join, [1tr in each of next 6 sts, 2tr in next st] around, 1tr in each of last 6 sts, join with ss in top of first ch-3. (96 sts)
Fasten off D.

Rnd 9: Attach A in any st, ch3, 1tr in same st as join, [1tr in each of next 7 sts, 2tr in next st] around, 1tr in each of last 7 sts, join with ss in top of first ch-3. (108 sts)
Fasten off A.

Rnd 10: Attach B in any st, ch3, 1tr in same st as join, [1tr in each of next 8 sts, 2tr in next st] around, 1tr in each of last 8 sts, join with ss in top of first ch-3. (120 sts)
Fasten off B.

Finishing
(work through both layers throughout)
Holding front and back with WS together, join C in any st, ch1, 1dc through both sts of each matching pair on front and back around (noting that there are 8 more sts on front than on back – miss every 16th st on front). Halfway around cushion, insert cushion pad and continue joining around. Ss in first dc to close.

Shell Edging
Attach D in any st, ch1, 1dc in same st, *miss 1 st, 5tr in next st, miss 1 st, 1dc in next st; rep from * around entire cushion, ss in first dc to close.

mini squares mug cosy

Dress up your mugs with a decorative and functional cosy. Using bright colours and sweet mini granny squares, these cosies will make your mugs the most stylish in town. They also work beautifully for slipping around those too-hot-to-handle takeaway coffee cups – keep one in your handbag for just such occasions.

Skill level: Easy

Materials

55% merino/33% microfibre/12% cashmere DK (light worsted) yarn, such as Debbie Bliss Cashmerino DK

* 1/2 x 50g ball (approx 55m/60yd) each in teal (A) and cream (B)
* 4.0mm (US size G/6) crochet hook
* Small button

Dimensions

* Length 22cm (8 1/2in), width 6cm (2 1/4in), to fit a mug 8cm (3in) diameter and 9.5cm (3 3/4in) high. Edging can be expanded to fit a larger mug.
* Exact tension is not important on this project.

Note

Join squares in a line either using the join-as-you-go method (see page 121) on second round after completing first square, or by seaming together with ss or dc join at point indicated in pattern.

Mini Granny Squares

(make 4)
Using A, ch4, join with ss in first ch to form a ring.
Rnd 1: Ch2, 2htr in ring, *ch2, 3htr in ring; rep from * 2 times more, ch2, join with ss in top of ch-2.
Fasten off A.
Rnd 2: Join B in any ch-2 sp, ch2, [2htr, ch2, 3htr] in same sp as join, *ch1, [3htr, ch2, 3htr] in next sp; rep from * 2 times more, ch1, join with ss in top of ch-2.
Fasten off B.
Seam four squares together using a ss or dc join, if join-as-you go method hasn't been used.

Edging Row

Join A in corner sp at start of one long edge of rectangle, ch2, 1htr in same sp as join, *[miss 2 sts, 3htr in next st] to next corner, [2htr, ch2, 2htr] in corner sp; rep from * around entire rectangle, omitting last corner rep, 2htr in same place as join, ch2, join with ss in top of ch-2. Do not fasten off.
Work button loop:
Turn work and, working down short side of rectangle, ss in each st until centre st is reached, ss in centre st, ch4, ss in same st as last ss, cont in ss to end of short side.
Fasten off.

Finishing

Weave in all ends.
Sew button to short side without button loop.

sunrise and flower potholders

This pretty potholder set is a perfect housewarming or birthday gift for the keen cook in your life. A double layer of crochet provides insulation against hot pans, and the colours can be coordinated to match any kitchen. They're attractive enough to display, so they can always be on hand when needed.

Skill level: Intermediate

Materials for both potholders

70% acrylic/30% wool Aran (worsted) yarn, such as Sirdar Click Aran with Wool

* 1 x 50g ball (approx 100m/108yd) in pink (A)

70% acrylic/30% alpaca Aran (worsted) yarn, such as Bernat Alpaca

* 1 x 50g ball (approx 110m/120yd) in cream (B)

* 5.0mm (US size H/8) crochet hook

Dimensions

* Sunrise Potholder: 23cm (9in) wide at widest point, 13.5cm (5¼in) tall at tallest point.

* Flower in a Frame Potholder: 17cm (6¾in) square.

* Exact tension is not important on this project.

sunrise potholder

Front
Do not work in the round and do not turn work.
Using A, ch4, join with ss in first ch to form a ring.
Row 1: Ch2, 2-tr cluster in ring, *ch2, 3-tr cluster in ring; rep from * 2 times more. (4 clusters)
Fasten off A.
Row 2: Attach B in ch-2 sp between first 2 clusters, ch2, [2-tr cluster, ch2, 3-tr cluster] in same sp, *ch2, [3-tr cluster, ch2, 3-tr cluster] in next ch-2 sp; rep from * one time more.
Fasten off B.
Row 3: Attach A in ch-2 sp between first 2 clusters, ch2, [2-tr cluster, ch2, 3-tr cluster] in same sp, *ch2, [3-tr cluster, ch2, 3-tr cluster] in next ch-2 sp; rep from * 3 times more.
Fasten off A.
Row 4: Attach B in ch-2 sp between first 2 clusters, ch2, [2-tr cluster, ch2, 3-tr cluster] in same sp, *ch2, 3-tr cluster in next ch-2 sp, ch2, [3-tr cluster, ch2, 3-tr cluster] in next ch-2 sp; rep from * 3 times more.
Fasten off B.
Row 5: Attach A in ch-2 sp between first 2 clusters, ch2, [2-tr cluster, ch2, 3-tr cluster] in same sp, *[ch2, 3-tr cluster in next ch-2 sp] 2 times, ch2, [3-tr cluster, ch2, 3-tr cluster] in next ch-2 sp; rep from * 3 times more.
Fasten off A.

Back
Using A, ch4, join with ss in first ch to form a ring.
Row 1: Ch3, 7tr in ring, turn.
Row 2: Ch3, 1tr in first tr, 2tr in each st to end, turn.
Row 3: Ch3, 2tr in next st, *1tr in next st, 2tr in next st; rep from * to end, turn.
Row 4: Ch3, 1tr in next st, 2tr in next st, *1tr in each of next 2 sts, 2tr in next st, rep from * to end, turn.
Row 5: Ch3, 1tr in each of next 2 sts, 2tr in next st, *1tr in each of next 3 sts, 2tr in next st; rep from * to end, turn.
Row 6: Ch2, 1htr in each of next 3 sts, 2htr in next st, *1htr in each of next 4 sts, 2htr in next st; rep from * to end.
Fasten off.

Finishing

Pin front and back WS together and work joining rnd through both layers throughout. (Note: there are fewer sts on back than on front. Joining rnd accounts for sts on front; on back miss

one fewer st between groups, as necessary, to fit evenly.)

Joining rnd: Attach B at start of straight edge, 1dc in each st/ch across straight edge, 2dc at corner, *miss 2 sts/chs, [3tr, ch3, ss in top of last tr, 2tr] in next st/ch, miss 2 sts/chs, 1dc in next st/ch; rep from * 5 times more, miss 2 sts/chs, [3tr, ch3, ss in top of last tr, 2tr] in next st/ch, miss 2 sts/chs, 2dc in last st, join with ss in first dc.

Weave in all ends.

flower in a frame potholder

Front

Using A, ch4, join with ss in first ch to form a ring.

Rnd 1: Ch2, 5-tr cluster in ring, *ch2, 6-tr cluster in ring, rep from * 2 times more, ch2, join with ss in top of first cluster.

Fasten off A.

Rnd 2: Attach B in any ch-2 sp, ch3, [2tr, ch2, 3tr] in same sp as join, *ch1, [3tr, ch2, 3tr] in next ch-2 sp; rep from * 2 times more, ch1, join with ss in top of ch-3.

Fasten off B.

Rnd 3: Attach A in any ch-2 corner sp, ch3, [2tr, ch2, 3tr] in same sp as join, *ch1, 3tr in next ch-1 sp, ch1, [3tr, ch2, 3tr] in next ch-2 corner sp; rep from * 2 times more, ch1, 3tr in next

ch-1 sp, ch1, join with ss in top of ch-3.

Fasten off A.

Rnd 4: Attach B in any ch-2 corner sp, ch3, [1tr, ch2, 2tr] in same sp as join, *1tr in each st and ch across side, [2tr, ch2, 2tr] in next corner sp; rep from * 2 times more, 1tr in each st and ch across last side, joining with ss in top of ch-3.

Fasten off B.

Rnd 5: Attach A in any ch-2 corner sp, ch3, [1tr, ch2, 2tr] in same sp as join, *miss next st, ss in next st, miss next 2 sts, [2tr, ch3, 2tr] in next st, miss next 2 sts, ss in next st, miss next 2 sts, [2tr, ch3, 2tr] in next st, miss next 2 sts, ss in next st, miss next st, [2tr, ch2, 2tr] in corner sp; rep from * 2 times more, miss next st, ss in next st, miss next 2 sts [2tr, ch3, 2tr] in next st, miss next 2 sts, ss in next st, miss next 2 sts, [2tr, ch3, 2tr] in next st, miss 2 sts, ss in next st, miss last st, join with ss in top of ch-3.

Fasten off A.

Rnd 6: Attach B in any ch-2 corner sp, ch3, [1tr, ch2, 2tr] in same sp as join, *[ch1, 3tr in next ss, ch1, ss in centre ch of ch-3] 2 times, ch1, 3tr in next ss, ch1, [2tr, ch2, 2tr] in corner sp; rep from * 2 times more, [ch1, 3tr in next ss, ch1, ss in centre ch of ch-3] 2 times, ch1, 3tr in last ss, ch1, join with ss in top of ch-3.

Fasten off B.

Back

Using A, ch4, join with ss in first ch to form a ring.

Rnd 1: Ch3, 2tr in ring, *ch2, 3tr in ring; rep from * 2 times more, ch2, join with ss in top of ch-3.

Rnd 2: Ch3, 1tr in each of next 2 tr, *[2tr, ch2, 2tr] in corner sp, 1tr in each of next 3 tr; rep from * 2 times more, [2tr, ch2,

2tr] in last corner sp, join with ss in top of ch-3.

Rnd 3: Ch3, 1tr in each of next 4 tr, *[2tr, ch2, 2tr] in corner sp, 1tr in each of next 7 tr; rep from * 2 times more, [2tr, ch2, 2tr] in corner sp, 1tr in each of next 2 tr, join with ss in top of ch-3.

Rnd 4: Ch3, 1tr in each of next 6 tr, *[2tr, ch2, 2tr] in corner sp, 1tr in each of next 11 tr; rep from * 2 times more, [2tr, ch2, 2tr] in corner sp, 1tr in each of next 3 tr, join with ss in top of ch-3.

Rnd 5: Ch3, 1tr in each of next 8 tr, *[2tr, ch2, 2tr] in corner sp, 1tr in each of next 15 tr; rep from * 2 times more, [2tr, ch2, 2tr] in corner sp, 1tr in each of next 5 tr, join with ss in top of ch-3.

Rnd 6: Ch1, *1dc in each st across side, [2dc, ch2, 2dc] in corner sp; rep from * around entire square, join with ss in first dc.

Fasten off.

Finishing

Place front and back WS together and work joining rnd through both layers throughout.

Joining rnd: Using A, join in any corner sp, ch1, [2dc, ch6, 2dc] in same sp as join, *1dc in each st and ch across side; rep from * around entire square, [2dc, ch6, 2dc] in each corner sp, join with ss in first dc.

Fasten off.

Weave in all ends.

granny stripes tea cosy

This clean, modern tea cosy has bags of style. It can easily be buttoned on and off and button loops can be lengthened or shortened and rows added or subtracted to fit your own teapot. Debbie Bliss Cashmerino is machine-washable and comes in a variety of gorgeous colours; use a machine-washable DK-weight yarn if you decide to substitute.

Skill level: Intermediate

Materials

55% merino/33% microfibre/12% cashmere DK (light worsted) yarn, such as Debbie Bliss Cashmerino DK

* ¹/₂ × 50g ball (approx 55m/60yd) each in deep blue (A), cream (B), deep pink (C), pale pink (D), pale grey (E), lilac (F)
* 4.0mm (US size G/6) crochet hook

Dimensions

* Cosy was worked to fit a teapot with a 50cm (20in) circumference at the widest point and 16cm (6¹/₄in) tall from bottom of pot to lid. Use the notes added throughout pattern to customize to fit your own teapot.
* Exact tension is not important on this project.

Notes

* Do NOT turn work between rows; start at beginning of row on same side each time.
* Try cosy on teapot at intervals, adding or subtracting rows as necessary to adjust for height.

Squares

(make two)
Start at base of teapot.
Using A, ch51.
Row 1: Miss first ch, 1dc in each ch.
Fasten off A.
Row 2: Attach B in first dc, ch3, 2tr in same st as join, *miss next 2 dc, 3tr in next dc; rep from * to end.
Fasten off B.
Row 3: Attach C in top of ch-3 from row below, ch3, *3tr in sp between tr groups; rep from * ending 2tr in top of last tr.
Fasten off C.
Row 4: Attach D in sp between ch-3 and first tr group from row below, ch3, 1tr in same sp, *3tr in sp between tr groups; rep from * ending 1tr in top of last tr.
Fasten off D.
Rep Rows 3 and 4 four times more (or height needed to widest point of teapot), changing colour each row.
Decrease for top:
Row 13: Attach A in sp between ch-3 and first tr from row below, ch3, *2tr in sp between tr groups; rep from * ending 1tr in top of last tr.
Fasten off A.
Row 14: Attach B in sp between ch-3 and first 2-tr group from row below, ch3, 1tr in same sp, *2tr in sp between 2-tr groups; rep from * ending 2tr in sp

between last 2-tr group and last tr.
Fasten off B.

Edging

Weave in all ends.
Working down one side of square, attach A, ch1, 1dc in same place as join, ch4, 1dc in same place as last dc (button loop made), work dc evenly down first side of square (cosy in photograph used 25dc).
Fasten off yarn.
Work edging on other side of square so there is a button loop at the diagonal corner. Lengthen button loops if your teapot is wider in circumference.

Finishing

Fit both sides of cosy to teapot and sew buttons to corners to match position of button loops.

stripes lampshade cover

When the lamp is off, this lampshade gives an inviting retro feel to any room. But when the lamp is on, the granny stripes and fanwork in the design glow like stained glass, beautifully illuminating each stitch.

Lampshade

Using B, ch79, join with ss in first ch to form a ring.

Rnd 1: Ch1, 1dc in each ch, join with ss in first dc.

Rnd 2: Ch3, 2tr in same st, *miss 2 sts, 3tr in next st; rep from * to end, join with ss in top of ch-3.

Rnd 3: Ss to next sp between tr groups, ch3, 2tr in same sp, *3tr in next sp; rep from * to end, join with ss in top of ch-3.

Rnd 4: Rep Rnd 3.

Rnd 5: Attach A in any sp between tr groups, ch3, 2tr in same sp, *3tr in next sp; rep from * to end, join with ss in top of ch-3.

Rnds 6–7: Rep Rnd 3.

Rep Rnds 5–7 using B. (9 rows of stripes 3 x B, 3 x A, 3 x B)

Bottom fan edging:

Attach A in any st, ch1, *[1dc in each of next 2 sts, 2dc in next st] 9 times, 1dc in each of next 3 sts; rep from * once more, join with ss in first dc. (96 sts)

Fan edging rnd 1: Ch1, 1dc in same st, *miss 2 sts, 5tr in next st, miss 2 sts, 1dc in next st; rep from * to end, omitting dc at end of last rep, join with ss in first dc.

Fan edging rnd 2: Ch3, 4tr in same st as join, *1dc in centre st of next 5-tr group, 5tr in next dc; rep from * ending 1dc in centre of next 5-tr group, join with ss in top of ch-3.

Top fan edging:

Turn work upside down. Attach B in any ch, ch1, 1dc in each ch around, join with ss in first dc.

Fan pattern rnd 1: Ch1, 1dc in same st, *miss 2 sts, 5tr in next st, miss 2 sts, 1dc in next st; rep from * to end, omitting dc at end of last rep, join with ss in top of first dc.

Fan pattern rnd 2: Ch3, 4tr in same st as join, *1dc in centre st of next 5-tr group, 5tr in next dc; rep ending 1dc in centre st of last tr-5 group, join with ss in top of ch-3.

Fan pattern rnd 3: Ss in each of 3 sts, ch1, 1dc in same st, *5tr in next dc, 1dc in centre st of next 5-tr group; rep from * omitting dc at end of last rep, join with ss in first dc.

Fasten off.

Finishing

Weave in all ends.

Skill level: Intermediate

Materials

100% extra fine merino wool DK (light worsted) yarn, such as Sublime Extra Fine Merino Wool DK

* 1 x 50g ball (approx 116m/127yd) in blue (A)

  75% merino/20% silk/5% cashmere lightweight Aran (light worsted) yarn, such as Sublime Cashmere Merino Silk Aran

* 1 x 50g ball (approx 86m/94yd) in yellow (B)

* 4.0mm (US size G/6) crochet hook

Dimensions

* To fit a lampshade frame 15cm (6in) high; top diameter 15cm (6in); bottom diameter 20cm (8in).

* Exact tension is not important on this project.

big squares ottoman cover

Liven up a boring ottoman with a smart granny square cover that is easy to make from oversized squares. This project is worked in only one colour to keep the lines clean and minimal – but if you prefer you could use a selection of colours.

Skill level: Easy

Materials

70% acrylic/30% wool Aran (worsted) yarn, such as Sirdar Click Aran with Wool

* 8 x 50g balls (approx 800m/864yd) in pink
* 5.5mm (US size 1/9) crochet hook

Dimensions

* To fit an ottoman approx 39cm (15¹/₂in) square. Other sizes can be made to fit by working more or fewer rounds.
* Exact tension is not important on this project.

Square

(make 5)
Ch4, join with ss in first ch to form a ring.

Rnd 1: Ch3, 2tr in ring, ch2, *3tr in ring, ch2; rep from * 2 times more, join with ss in top of ch-3.

Rnd 2: Ss in first 2-tr and in first ch of corner sp, ch3, [2tr, ch2, 3tr] in same sp, *ch1, [3tr, ch2, 3tr] in next ch-2 sp; rep from * 2 times more, ch1, join with ss in top of ch-3.

Rnd 3: Ss in first 2-tr and in first ch of corner sp, ch3, [2tr, ch2, 3tr] in same sp, *ch1, 3tr in next ch-1 sp, ch1, [3tr, ch2, 3tr] in next ch-2 sp; rep from * 2 times more, ch1, 3tr in next ch-1 sp, ch1, join with ss in top of ch-3.

Rnd 4: Ss in first 2-tr and in first ch of corner sp, ch3, [2tr, ch2, 3tr] in same sp, *[ch1, 3tr] in each ch-1 sp, ch1, [3tr, ch2, 3tr] in next ch-2 sp; rep from * 2 times more, [ch1, 3tr] in each ch-1 sp, ch1, join with ss in top of ch-3.
Rep Rnd 4 eight times more, or to size desired.

Finishing

Use dc to join squares to form cube shape with open base.

flower garden table mats

Make a delightful flower garden to brighten up your kitchen table! Worked in cheerful pastels, this matching placemat and drinks coaster will make your table feel like springtime all year round.

Skill level: Intermediate

Materials

100% cotton No.5 crochet cotton, such as DMC Petra Crochet Cotton Perle No.5

* 1 × 100g ball (400m/685yd) in green (MC) per mat + coaster

* Small amounts of pink, peach, lilac and blue (CC)

* 2.5mm (US size C/2) crochet hook

Dimensions

* Mat approx 40 × 30cm (16 × 12in); coaster approx 10cm (4in).

* Exact tension is not important on this project.

Table Placemat Square

Using any CC, ch4, join with ss in first ch to form a ring.

Rnd 1: Ch1, 12dc in centre of ring, join with ss in first dc.

Rnd 2: [Ch4, miss 2 sts, 1dc in next st] 3 times, ch4, miss last 2 dc, join with ss at base of first ch-4. (4 petal spaces)

Rnd 3: [1dc, 1htr, 4tr, 1htr, 1dc] in each ch-4 petal space, join with ss in first dc.

Rnd 4: Attach MC in 2nd of 4 tr on any petal, ch3, [2tr, ch2, 3tr] in same st, *ch1, 3tr in next dc, ch1, [3tr, ch2, 3tr] in 2nd of 4 tr on next petal; rep from * 2 times more, ch1, 3tr in next dc, ch1, join with ss in top of ch-3.

Rnd 5: Ss to first ch-2 corner sp, ch3, [2tr, ch2, 3tr] in same sp, *[ch1, 3tr] in each ch-1 sp, ch1, [3tr, ch2, 3tr] in next corner sp; rep from * 2 times more, [ch1, 3tr] in each ch-1 sp, ch1, join with ss in top of ch-3.

Rep Rnd 5 two times more.

Fasten off.

Work another 11 squares as starting square, but use join-as-you-go method (see page 121) on last rnd, arranging squares 4 squares across by 3 squares down. Change centre CC each time if desired.

Drinks Coaster Granny Pentagon

Using any CC, ch5, join with ss in first ch to form a ring.

Rnd 1: Ch1, 15dc in centre of ring, join with ss in first dc.

Rnd 2: [Ch4, miss 2 sts, 1dc in next st] 4 times, ch4, join with ss at base of first ch-4. (5 petal spaces)

Rnd 3: [1dc, 1htr, 4tr, 1htr, 1dc] in each ch-4 petal space, join with ss in first dc.

Rnd 4: Attach MC in 2nd of 4 tr on any petal, ch3, [2tr, ch2, 3tr] in same st, *ch1, 3tr in next dc, ch1, [3tr, ch2, 3tr] in 2nd of 4 tr on next petal; rep from * 3 times more, ch1, 3tr next dc, ch1, join with ss in top of first ch-3.

Rnd 5: Ss to first ch-2 corner sp, ch3, [2tr, ch2, 3tr] in same sp, *[ch1, 3tr] in each ch-1 sp, ch1, [3tr, ch2, 3tr] in next corner sp; rep from * 3 times more, [ch1, 3tr] in each ch-1 sp, ch1, join with ss in top of ch-3.

Rep Rnd 5 once more.

Fasten off.

Finishing

Weave in all ends.

granny hexagon table runner

Worked in precise geometric shapes and one colour, this clean and unfussy runner redefines the 'doily' into a stylish table centrepiece. You can easily make it longer by adding more hexagons to each strip, or wider by adding another strip.

Skill level: Intermediate

Materials

100% cotton No.5 crochet cotton, such as DMC Petra Crochet Cotton Perle No.5

* 1 x 100g ball (400m/685yd) in pink
* 2.5mm (US size C/2) crochet hook

Dimensions

* Runner is 12 hexagons long and 3 across, or desired size.
* Exact tension is not important on this project.

Starting Hexagon

Ch6, join with ss in first ch to form a ring.

Rnd 1: Ch3, 1tr in ring, *ch2, 2tr in ring; rep from * 4 times more, ch2, join with ss in top of ch-3.

Rnd 2: Ss to first ch-2 sp, ch3, [1tr, ch2, 2tr] in sp, *ch1, [2tr, ch2, 2tr] in next ch-2 sp; rep from * 4 times more, ch1, join with ss in top of ch-3.

Rnd 3: Ss to first ch-2 sp, ch3, [1tr, ch2, 2tr] in sp, *ch1, 2tr in next ch-1 sp, ch1, [2tr, ch2, 2tr] in next ch-2 sp; rep from * 4 times more, ch1, 2tr in next ch-1 sp, ch1, join with ss in top of ch-3.

Rnd 4: Ss to first ch-2 sp, ch3, [1tr, ch2, 2tr] in sp, *[ch1, 2tr in ch-1 sp] 2 times, ch1, [2tr, ch2, 2tr] in next ch-2 sp; rep from * 4 times more, [ch1, 2tr in ch-1 sp] 2 times, ch1, join with ss in top of ch-3.
Fasten off.

Work rem 11 hexagons of first strip as starting hexagon, but use join-as-you-go method (see page 121) in Rnd 4 for one side of hexagon.
Work second and third strip of 11 hexagons as starting hexagon, but use the join-as-you-go method in Rnd 4 for one corner of first hexagon of each strip, then one side on one corner of rem hexagons.

Finishing

Weave in all ends.

cotton square flannels

A pop of bright colour around the edge of these cotton flannels can be coordinated to match your bathroom. Imagine giving these in a gift basket with luxurious bath salts and soaps.

Flannel

Using A, ch4, join with ss in first ch to form a ring.

Rnd 1: Ch3, 2tr in ring, *ch2, 3tr in ring; rep from * 2 times more, ch2, join with ss in top of ch-3.

Rnd 2: Ch3, *1tr in each tr to next corner sp, [2tr, ch2, 2tr] in corner sp; rep from * 3 times more, join with ss in top of ch-3.

Rnd 3: Ch3, *1tr in each tr to next corner sp, [2tr, ch2, 2tr] in corner sp; rep from * 3 times more, 1tr in each st to end, join with ss in top of ch-3.

Rep Rnd 3 four times more.

Fasten off A.

Rnd 8: Attach B in any st, ch2, 1htr in next st and each st and ch around flannel, join with ss in top of ch-2.

Fasten off B.

Rnd 9: Attach A in any st, ch1, 1dc in same st and each st around flannel, work 2dc in each of 2 corner sts, join with ss in first dc.

Fasten off.

Finishing

Weave in all ends.

Skill level: Easy

Materials

100% organic cotton Aran (worsted) yarn, such as Debbie Bliss Eco Aran

* 1 x 50g ball (approx 75m/82yd) in ecru (A)

* Small amount DK (light worsted) or Aran (worsted) cotton yarn in blue or orange (B)

* 5.0mm (US size H/8) crochet hook

Dimensions

* Approx 24cm (9¹/₂in) square.

* Exact tension is not important on this project.

granny square cushion cover

As vivid as boiled sweets, this gorgeous cushion cover will add style to any room – choose colours that complement your décor. You can use any DK-weight cotton you happen to have already and the cushion cover is removable for washing. This is a simple project and a great introduction to granny squares.

Skill level: Easy

Materials

100% cotton yarn, such as Rowan Hand Knit Cotton

* 1 × 50g ball (85m/93yd) in each of green, dark blue, light pink, dark pink
* 2 × 50g balls (170m/186yd) in red

100% cotton DK (light worsted) yarn, such as Debbie Bliss Cotton DK

* 1 × 50g ball (84m/92yd) in each of medium blue and light blue
* 4.5mm (US size 7) crochet hook
* 41–46cm (16–18in) cushion pad
* 65cm (25½in) of 22mm (⅞in) satin ribbon

Dimensions

* To fit a 41–46cm (16–18in) cushion pad.
* Exact tension is not important on this project.

Notes

* Both front and back piece should be slightly smaller than cushion pad, so it stretches to fit closely.
* Ribbon can be removed for washing.

Front of Cushion Cover

Starting square:

Using any colour, ch4, join with ss in first ch to form a ring.

Rnd 1: Ch3, 2tr in ring, *ch2, 3tr in ring; rep from * 2 times more, ch2, join with ss in top of ch-3.

Rnd 2: Attach second colour in any corner sp, ch3, [2tr, ch2, 3tr] in same sp, *ch1, [3tr, ch2, 3tr] in next corner sp; rep from * 2 times more, ch1, join with ss in top of ch-3.

Rnd 3: Attach third colour in any corner sp, ch3, [2tr, ch2, 3tr] in same sp, *ch1, 3tr in next sp, ch1, [3tr, ch2, 3tr] in next corner sp; rep from * 2 times more, ch1, 3tr in next sp, ch1, join with ss in top of ch-3.

Fasten off.

Make 24 more squares the same way, but using the join-as-you-go technique (see page 121) on Rnd 3 to form a 5 x 5 square of squares.

Back of Cushion Cover

Using red, ch4, join with ss in first ch to form a ring.

Rnd 1: Ch3, 2tr in ring, *ch2, 3tr in ring; rep from * 2 times more, ch2, join with ss in top of ch-3.

Rnd 2: Ss in each of next 2 tr and first ch of corner sp, ch3, [2tr, ch2, 3tr] in same sp, *ch1, [3tr, ch2, 3tr] in next corner sp; rep from * 2 times more, ch1, join with ss in top of ch-3.

Rnd 3: Ss in each of next 2 tr and first ch of corner sp, ch3, [2tr, ch2, 3tr] in same sp, *ch1, 3tr in next sp, ch1, [3tr, ch2, 3tr] in next corner sp; rep from * 2 times more, ch1, 3tr in next sp, ch1, join with ss in top of ch-3.

Rnd 4: Ss in each of next 2 tr and first ch of corner sp,

ch3, [2tr, ch2, 3tr] in same sp, *ch1, [3tr in next sp, ch1] to next corner, [3tr, ch2, 3tr] in next corner sp; rep from * 2 times more, ch1, [3tr in next sp, ch1] to end, join with ss in top of ch-3.

Rep Rnd 4 for another 7 rnds.

Changing colour every round, work 3 more rounds.

Last rnd: Change colour and use the join-as-you-go technique on last rnd of back to attach it on 3 sides to front. Finish the last side of back without joining to front.

Fasten off.

Finishing

Weave in all ends. Insert cushion pad through open side. Cut the ribbon into four equal lengths, thread lengths through open side at intervals and tie closed. Seal ends of ribbon with a dab of glue to prevent fraying.

puffed square lap quilt

This little quilt is perfect to snuggle across your lap on a cold evening. It's constructed of closed granny squares and stuffed with toy stuffing, which gives it its extra-insulated warmth. The patchwork effect is achieved both by using a variegated yarn and substituting solids in complementary colours for some squares.

Stuffed Square

Using any colour, ch4, join with ss in first ch to form a ring.

Rnd 1: Ch3, 2tr in ring, *ch2, 3tr in ring; rep from * 2 times more, ch2, join with ss in top of ch-3.

Rnd 2: Ch3, *1tr in each tr to next corner sp, [2tr, ch2, 2tr] in next corner sp; rep from * 3 times more, join with ss in top of ch-3.

Rnd 3: Ch3, *1tr in each tr to next corner sp, [2tr, ch2, 2tr] in corner sp; rep from * 3 times more, 1tr in each rem st, join with ss in top of ch-3.

Rep Rnd 3 once more.

Fasten off.

Finishing

Make another square as above. With WS facing, join 3 sides with dc join, working [1dc, ch1, 1dc] in each corner. Stuff lightly and join last side with dc join, ss in first dc. Fasten off.

Make 15 more stuffed squares (16 stuffed squares total) and arrange in four rows of four squares to form a large square. Join squares together using dc join.

Popcorn Stitch Edging

Attach multi pink yarn in any st, ch3, 4tr in same st, remove hook from loop, insert hook in top of ch-3 and back into loop, yrh and pull through loop and st (popcorn made), *ch1, miss 1 st, 5tr in next st, remove hook from loop, insert hook in top of first of 5-tr and back into loop, yrh and pull through loop and st (popcorn made); rep from * around entire piece, working 3 popcorns in each corner without missing st between popcorns.

Weave in all ends.

Skill level: Advanced

Materials

100% wool chunky (bulky) weight yarn, such as Patons Eco Wool Chunky

* 6 × 50g balls (approx 480m/522yd) in multi pink

70% acrylic/30% alpaca Aran (worsted) yarn, such as Bernat Natural Blends Alpaca

* 1 × 50g ball (approx 110m/120yd) in each of light pink and cream

70% acrylic/30% wool Aran (worsted) yarn, such as Sirdar Click Aran with Wool

* 2 × 50g balls (approx 200m/216yd) in medium pink

* Various scraps of heavy Aran (worsted) or chunky (bulky) weight yarn, and DK (light worsted) weight yarn held double

* 6.0mm (US size J/10) crochet hook

* 1 bag of fibrefill toy stuffing

Dimensions

* Each square measures 15cm (6in); quilt measures 65cm (25 1/2in) square.

* Exact tension is not important on this project.

sunflower square seat cover

Add some beautiful blooms to your kitchen chairs! A central sunflower motif is surrounded by smaller flowers in this removable cover made from hard-wearing cotton yarn that can be washed over and over for practicality.

Skill level: Advanced

Materials

100% cotton DK (light worsted) yarn, such as Debbie Bliss Cotton DK

* 1 x 50g ball (84m/92yd) in brown (A)
* 4 x 50g balls (336m/368yd) in white (C)

100% organic cotton Aran (worsted) yarn, such as Debbie Bliss Eco Aran

* 2 x 50g balls (approx 150m/164yd) in yellow (B)
* 4.5mm (US size 7) crochet hook
* 38cm (15in) seat cushion, white or colour desired
* 160cm (63in) of 1.5cm (⅝in) grosgrain ribbon

Dimensions

* To fit a 38cm (15in) seat cushion.
* Exact tension is not important on this project.

Central Motif

Using A, ch4, join with ss in first ch to form a ring.

Rnd 1: Ch3, 11tr in ring, join with ss in top of ch-3. (12 sts)

Rnd 2: Ch3, 1tr in same st as join, 2tr in each st around, join with ss in top of ch-3. (24 sts)
Fasten off.

First petal:

Row 1: Attach B in any st, ch1, 1dc in same st and each of next 2 sts, turn. (3 sts)

Row 2: Ch1, 2dc in first st, 1dc in next st, 2dc in last st, turn. (5 sts)

Row 3: Ch1, 1dc in each st, turn. (5 sts)

Row 4: Rep Row 3.

Row 5: Ch1, dc2tog, 1dc in next st, dc2tog, turn. (3 sts)

Row 6: Ch1, 1dc in each st, turn. (3 sts)

Row 7: Ch1, dc3tog, turn. (1 st)

Row 8: Ch1, 1dc in dc.
Fasten off.
Rep Rows 1–8 for each petal, joining B in next st after previous petal. (8 petals total)

Flower edging:

Rnd 1: Attach C in tip of any petal, ch3, [2tr, ch2, 3tr] in same sp, *ch7, [3tr, ch2, 3tr] in next petal tip; rep from * to end, ch7, join with ss in top of ch-3.

Rnd 2: Ss to next ch-2 sp, ch3, [2tr, ch2, 3tr] in same sp, *ch3, 3tr in 4th ch of 7, ch3, [3tr, ch2, 3tr] in next ch-2 sp; rep from * ending ch3, 3tr in 4th ch of 7, ch3, join with ss in top of ch-3.
Fasten off.

Rnd 3: Attach B, to any 2-ch sp, ch4, [2dtr, ch2, 3dtr] in same sp (corner worked), *ch2, 3tr in 2nd ch of 3, ch2, 3htr in 2nd ch of 3, ch4, 2dc in next 2-ch sp, ch4, 3htr in 2nd ch of 3, ch2, 3tr in 2nd ch of 3, ch2, [3dtr, ch2, 3dtr] in next ch-2 sp (corner worked); rep from * to end omitting corner at end of last rep, join with ss in top of first ch-4.

Rnd 4: Ss to next corner sp, ch4, [2dtr, ch2, 3dtr] in same sp (corner worked), *[ch1, 3tr in next sp] 2 times, ch1, 3htr in next sp, 1dc in 2nd dc from rnd below, 3htr in next sp, [ch1, 3tr in next sp] 2 times, ch1, [3dtr, ch2, 3dtr] in next corner sp (corner worked); rep from * to end omitting corner at end of last rep, join with ss in top of first ch-4.
Fasten off.

Starting Border Square

Using A, ch5, join with ss in first ch to form a ring.

Rnd 1: Ch1, 12dc in ring, join with ss in first dc.
Fasten off.

Rnd 2: Attach B in any st, *ch3, miss 2 sts, ss in next st; rep from * to end working last ss in same st as join. (4 petal loops)

Rnd 3: [1dc, 1htr, 1tr, 2dtr, 1tr, 1htr, 1dc] in each 3-ch sp around, join with ss in first dc. Fasten off.

Rnd 4: Attach C in first dtr of any petal, ch3, [2tr, ch2, 3tr] in same sp, *ch1, 3dtr in last dc of same petal, ch1, [3tr, ch2, 3tr] in first dtr next petal; rep from * 2 times more, ch1, 3dtr last dc of same petal, ch1, join with ss in top of ch-3. Fasten off.

Make 15 more border squares as starting border square but using join-as-you-go technique (see page 121) on Rnd 4 to form a frame around central motif. (5 squares on each side) Using B, attach border squares to central motif using dc join.

Back

Using C, ch4, join with ss in first ch to form a ring.

Rnd 1: Ch3, 2tr in ring, *ch2, 3tr in ring; rep from * 2 times more, ch2, join with ss in top of ch-3.

Rnd 2: Ss to next ch-2 sp, ch3, [2tr, ch2, 3tr] in same sp, *ch1, [3tr, ch2, 3tr] in next corner sp; rep from * 2 times more, ch1, join with ss in top of ch-3.

Rnd 3: Ss to next ch-2 sp, ch3, [2tr, ch2, 3tr] in same sp, *ch1, 3tr in next sp, ch1, [3tr, ch2, 3tr] in next corner sp; rep from * 2 times more, ch1, 3tr in next sp, ch1, join with ss in top of ch-3.

Rnd 4: Ss to next ch-2 sp, ch3, [2tr, ch2, 3tr] in same sp, *ch1, [3tr in next sp, ch1] to next corner, [3tr, ch2, 3tr] in corner sp; rep from * 2 times more, ch1, [3tr in next sp, ch1] to end, join with ss in top of ch-3.

Rep Rnd 4 another 11 times, or make big enough to fit back of cushion. Fasten off.

Finishing

Weave in all ends.

Insert cushion between front and back layers. Cut ribbon into 8 equal lengths and use to tie front and back together at corners and middle of sides.

sweet granny bunting

This charming pastel bunting will brighten any space – imagine stringing it in the garden for a delightful tea party with tiny cakes and sandwiches, or hanging it in a corner of your office to give a lift to your work day. Worked in a luxurious merino/cashmere blend, this yarn has a luscious sheen and is a dream to crochet. Vary the colours to reflect your own style!

Skill level: Easy

Materials

75% merino/20% silk/5% cashmere lightweight Aran (light worsted) yarn, such as Sublime Cashmere Merino Silk Aran

* 1 x 50g ball (approx 86m/94yd) in each of pale blue, lilac and pale pink
* 4.0mm (US size G/6) crochet hook

Dimensions

* Each triangle side approx 15cm (6in).
* Exact tension is not important on this project.

Bunting Triangles
(make as many as desired)
Using any colour, ch4, join with ss in first ch to form a ring.
Rnd 1: Ch3, 2tr in ring, [ch3, 3tr in ring] 2 times, ch3, join with ss in top of ch-3.
Fasten off first colour.
Rnd 2: Attach second colour in any ch-3 sp, ch3, [2tr, ch2, 3tr] all in same sp as join, *ch2, [3tr ch2, 3tr] in next ch-3 sp; rep from * once more, ch2, join with ss in top of ch-3.
Fasten off second colour.
Rnd 3: Attach third colour in any ch-3 corner sp, ch3, [2tr, ch3, 3tr] all in same sp as join, *ch2, 3tr in next sp, ch2, [3tr, ch3, 3tr] in next ch-3 corner sp; rep from * once more, ch2, 3tr in next sp, ch2, join with ss in top of ch-3.
Fasten off third colour.
Rnd 4: Attach first colour in any ch-3 corner sp, ch3, [2tr, ch3, 3tr] all in same sp as join, *[ch2, 3tr in next sp] 2 times, ch2, [3tr, ch3, 3tr] in corner sp; rep from * once more, [ch2, 3tr in next sp] two times, ch2, join with ss in top of ch-3.
Fasten off first colour.

Edging rnd 1: Attach second colour in any st, 1dc in each st/ch around working 2dc in each of 3 ch in corners, join with ss in first dc, do not fasten off.
Edging rnd 2: *Miss 2 sts, 5htr in next st, miss 2 sts, ss in next st; rep from * around entire piece.
Fasten off.

Hanging Cord
Using any colour, ch20, *[1dc in each of third and fourth htr of next group of 5 htr from Edging rnd 2 on triangle, ch2] across one side of triangle, ch8; rep from * until all triangles are attached, ch18.
Fasten off.

Finishing
Weave in all ends.

white and bright bedcover

You'll be surprised at how fast this hybrid granny square/granny stripe blanket works up, and how addictive those speedy stripes are! Using the join-as-you-go method for the squares section means no more stacks of squares waiting forever to be joined. The combination of crisp white and eye-catching brights gives this blanket clean, modern appeal.

Skill level: Advanced

Materials

100% acrylic DK (light worsted) yarn, such as Patons FAB DK

* 8 x 100g balls (approx 2194m/2400yd) in white (A)

100% acrylic DK (light worsted) yarn, such as Stylecraft Special DK

* 600g approx total in assorted colours (B)

* 4.5mm (US size 7) crochet hook

Dimensions

* Each square measures 11cm (4¼in); bedcover measures 158cm (62in) square.

* Exact tension is not important on this project.

Note

* When working crab stitch edging, left-handed crocheters should insert hook into next st to left and then continue to work right to left.

Starting Square

Using any colour B, ch4, join with ss to form a ring.

Rnd 1: Ch3, 2tr in ring, *ch2, 3tr in ring; rep from * 2 times more, ch2, join with ss in top of ch-3.
Fasten off.

Rnd 2: Attach second colour in any corner sp, ch3, [2tr, ch2, 3tr] in same sp, *ch1, [3tr, ch2, 3tr] in next corner sp; rep from * 2 times more, ch1, join with ss in top of first ch-3.
Fasten off.

Rnd 3: Attach third colour in any corner sp, ch3, [2tr, ch2, 3tr] in same sp, *ch1, 3tr in next sp, ch1, [3tr, ch2, 3tr] in next corner sp; rep from * 2 times more, ch1, 3tr in next sp, ch1, join with ss in top of ch-3.

Rnd 4: Attach A in any corner sp, ch3, [2tr, ch2, 3tr] in same sp, *ch1, [3tr in next sp, ch1] 2 times, [3tr, ch2, 3tr] in next corner sp; rep from * 2 times more, ch1, [3tr in next sp, ch1] 2 times, join with ss in top of ch-3.
Fasten off.

Make 27 more squares using the join-as-you-go method (see page 121) on Rnd 4 to make 2 rows of 14 squares.

First Granny Stripe Section

Row 1: Attach A in corner sp at start of one long side of strip, ch3, 2tr in same sp, 3tr in every ch-1 sp and 3tr in joining place between squares to end, 3tr in last corner sp, turn.

Row 2: Ch3, 1tr in first tr, 3tr in each sp between tr-3 groups to end, 1tr in top of ch-3, turn.

Row 3: Ch3, 2tr sp before first tr-3 group, 3tr in each sp between tr-3 groups to end, 2tr in sp after last tr-3 group, 1tr in top of ch-3, turn.
Fasten off A.

Row 4: Using B, ch3, 1tr in first tr, 3tr in each sp between tr-3 groups to end, 1tr in top of ch-3.

Rep Rows 3 and 4, working in stripes of 3 rows of A, one row of B, 3 rows of A. Work another section of 2 rows each of 14 granny squares, using the join-as-you-go method (see page 121) in Rnd 4 of the first row of squares to attach to the granny stripe portion. Work second granny stripe section on other edge of second long strip of squares, alternating 3 rows of A with one row of B, until piece measures 154cm (60½in) or desired length. Fasten off.

Finishing
Weave in all ends.

Edging
Attach A to any st and work tr edging around entire piece, working [2tr, ch2, 2tr] in each corner sp. Attach B to any st and work crab st edging around entire bedcover working from left to right as follows: ch1, 1dc in same st, *insert hook into next st to right, 1dc; rep in each st around working 4 crab st in each corner sp. Left-handed crocheters see note on page 44.

squares **christmas stocking**

This traditional yet stylish pattern adds a cosy, homey feel to your holiday celebrations. Make a stocking for each member of the family – children can pick their own colours!

Skill level: Advanced

Materials

70% acrylic/30% wool DK (light worsted) yarn, such as Sirdar Click DK

* 1 x 50g ball (150m/164yd) in green (A)

63% wool/37% acrylic DK (light worsted) yarn, such as Patons Wool Blend DK

* 1 x 100g ball (approx 250m/274yd) in cream (B)
* 4.0mm (US size G/6) crochet hook

Dimensions

* Each square measures 10cm (4in); stocking width 20cm (8in); length from top edge to heel approx 37cm (14¼in).
* Exact tension is not important on this project.

Traditional Granny Square

(make 12)
Using A, ch4, join with ss in first ch to form a ring.
Rnd 1: Ch3, 2tr in ring *ch2, 3tr in ring; rep from * 2 times more, ch2, join with ss in top of ch-3.
Fasten off.
Rnd 2: Attach B in any corner sp, ch3, [2tr, ch2, 3tr] in same sp, *ch1, [3tr, ch2, 3tr] in next sp; rep from * 2 times more, ch1, join with ss in top of ch-3.
Fasten off.
Rnd 3: Attach A in any corner sp, ch3, [2tr, ch2, 3tr] in same sp, *ch1, 3tr in next sp, ch1, [3tr, ch2, 3tr] in next corner sp; rep from * 2 times more, ch1, 3tr in next sp, ch1, join with ss in top of ch-3.
Fasten off.

Stocking chart
Dotted lines indicate where to fold.

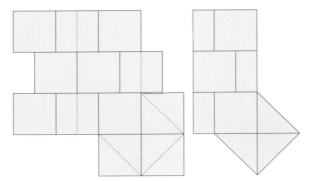

Rnd 4: Attach B in any corner sp, ch3, [2tr, ch2, 3tr] in same sp, *[ch1, 3tr in next sp] 2 times, ch1, [3tr, ch2, 3tr] in next corner sp; rep from * 2 times more, [ch1, 3tr in next sp] 2 times, ch1, join with ss in top of ch-3.
Fasten off.

Assemble squares in rows as shown on chart, far left. As indicated on chart, do not join last half of third square in second row to square below – this will allow you to fold back these squares on the dotted lines. Fold squares on left side back along vertical dotted fold line and squares at bottom diagonally back on the fold lines to create the stocking shape as shown left.

Finishing

Weave in all ends.
With WS together, work ss join through each st. Push point at heel inside stocking and stitch into place. Flatten stockings.

Side Edging

Using B, work a row of dc around entire outer edge, leaving top open, turn.
Next row: 1dc in first st, *miss 2 sts, 5tr in next st, miss 2 sts, 1dc in next st; rep from * around stocking (omitting top opening), missing only one st between tr groups and dc around corners.
Fasten off.

Top Edging

Attach B in any st of top opening, ch1, 1dc in same st and each st around, join with ss in first dc.
Rnd 2: Ch3, 2tr in st at base of ch, *miss 2 sts, 1dc in next st, miss 2 sts, 5tr in next st; rep from * ending miss 2 sts, 1dc in next st, miss 2 sts, 2tr in same place as first tr, join with ss in 3rd of 3 ch.
Rnd 3: Ch1, 1dc in same st as join, *5tr in next dc, 1dc in centre st of 5tr; rep from * omitting last dc, join with ss in first dc.
Rep Rnds 2 and 3 once, then work Rnd 2 again.
Last edging rnd: Work as Rnd 3, but work [2tr, ch3, ss in third ch from hook, 3tr] in place of 5tr.
Fasten off.

Hanging Tab

Attach B at back of top opening, ch8, ss in same place.
Fasten off.
Weave in all ends.

chapter 2

accessories

Drape yourself and your loved ones in cosy accessories that give
granny squares a contemporary twist, like fabulous striped arm
warmers, practical and lovely iPhone/iPad covers, and even
a warm coat for the family pooch! Why not crochet
up some quick-to-make bags, scarves, and
a gorgeous granny triangle shawl?

colourful clutch bag

When you need to add a burst of colour to an outfit, this clutch bag – just big enough for the essentials for an evening out – is the perfect accessory. Line with coordinating fabric for an extra kick. Made in scraps of DK-weight yarn, it's a great stash-buster.

Skill level: Easy

Materials

* Small amounts of any DK-weight (light worsted) yarn in at least eleven different colours, about 1 × 50g ball (137m/125yd) of yarn in total
* 4.0mm (US size G/6) crochet hook
* 25 × 30cm (10 × 12in) piece of cotton fabric
* Sewing needle and thread

Dimensions

* 20 × 9.5cm (8 × 3³/₄in) closed.
* Exact tension is not important on this project.

Notes:

* Join squares in a line either using the join-as-you-go method (see page 121) on second round after completing first square, or by seaming together with ss join at point indicated in pattern.
* When working bag pocket do NOT turn work between rows; start at beginning of row on same side each time.

Squares
(make 4)
Using first colour, ch4, join with ss in first ch to form a ring.
Rnd 1: Ch2, 2htr in ring, *ch2, 3htr in ring; rep from * 2 times more, ch2, join with ss in top of ch-2.
Fasten off first colour.
Rnd 2: Join second colour in any ch-2 corner sp, ch2, [2htr, ch2, 3htr] in same sp as join, *ch1, [3htr, ch2, 3htr] in next

corner sp; rep from * 2 times more, ch1, join with ss in top of ch-2.
Fasten off second colour.
Seam four squares together with ss join, if join-as-you go method hasn't been used.

Edging
Attach new colour in any sp and work 1dc in each st and ch around all 4 sides of rectangle, working 2dc in each corner sp.
Fasten off.

Bag Pocket
Work back and forth in rows to form striped bag.
Row 1: Attach new colour at corner of squares rectangle, ch2, 1htr in each st across long side of rectangle.
Row 2: Attach new colour to top of ch-2, 1htr in each htr across.
Rep Row 2 another 24 times or to achieve desired size of bag pocket.
Fasten off.

For small dogs:
(Approx 34–42cm/13$\frac{1}{2}$–16$\frac{1}{2}$in from base of tail to neck and approx 34cm/13$\frac{1}{2}$in around ribcage) follow chart A.

For medium dogs:
(Approx 46–53cm/18–21in long from base of tail to neck and approx 46cm/18in around ribcage) follow chart B.

For large dogs:
(Approx 57–65cm/22$\frac{1}{2}$–25$\frac{1}{2}$in long from base of tail to neck and approx 57cm/22$\frac{1}{2}$in around ribcage) follow chart C.

Finishing

If you need to adjust fit with ch loops, attach B at point marked O on diagram and work ch for double the required length, ss in same place as join.
Fasten off.
Weave in all ends.
Sew on buttons.

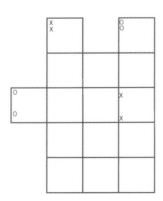

Chart A
Attach buttons at spots marked X.
Attach optional button loops at spots marked O.

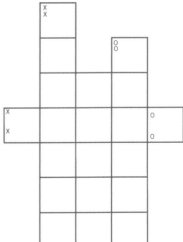

Chart B
Attach buttons at spots marked X.
Attach optional chain loops at spots marked O.

Chart C
Attach buttons at spots marked X.
Attach optional button loops at spots marked O.

crochet hook roll holder

Organize your crochet hooks in this practical and pretty holder. Granny squares form the decorative wrap, while a double layer of half treble crochet separated into slots keeps your hooks secure. A wider version could be made to store knitting needles.

Skill level: Intermediate

Materials

100% pure wool DK (light worsted) yarn, such as Rowan Pure Wool DK

* 2 x 50g balls (250m/274yd) in cream (A)

70% acrylic/30% wool DK (light worsted) yarn, such as Sirdar Click DK

* 1 x 50g ball (150m/164yd) in light blue (B)

55% merino/33% microfibre/12% cashmere DK (light worsted) yarn, such as Debbie Bliss Cashmerino DK

* 1 x 50g ball (approx 110m/120yd) in dark blue (C)
* 4.5mm (US size 7) crochet hook
* Optional: Length of 1.5cm (⅝in) grosgrain ribbon

Dimensions

* Each square measures 8.5cm (3⅜in); finished size of holder 26 x 35cm (10¼ x 13¾in)
* Exact tension is not important on this project.

Starting Square

Using C, ch4, join with ss in first ch to form a ring.

Rnd 1: Ch3, 2tr in ring, *ch2, 3tr in ring; rep from * 2 times more, ch2, join with ss in top of ch-3.

Rnd 2: Attach B in any corner sp, ch3, [2tr, ch2, 3tr] in same sp, *ch1, [3tr, ch2, 3tr] in next corner sp; rep from * 2 times more, ch1, join with ss in top of ch-3.

Rnd 3: Attach A in any corner sp, ch3, [2tr, ch2, 3tr] in same sp, *ch1, 3tr in next sp, ch1, [3tr, ch2, 3tr] in next corner sp; rep from * 2 times more, ch1, 3tr in next

sp, ch1, join with ss in top of ch-3. Fasten off.

Work two more squares as Starting square, but use the join-as-you-go method (see page 121) in Rnd 3 to make a strip of 3 squares.

Main Piece

Attach C in 2nd ch of ch-2 at start of one long edge of strip of 3 squares.

Row 1: Ch2, miss st at base of ch, 1htr in each st and ch, and 1htr in join between squares across long side of strip, turn. (41 sts)

Row 2: Ch2, miss st at base of ch, 1htr in each st to end, 1htr in top of ch-2, turn.

Rep last row 8 times more. Fasten off.

Attach B and work Row 2 ten times.

Fasten off.

Attach A and work Row 2 ten times.

Fasten off.

First Pocket Flap

Attach A to top left-hand corner, ch2, work 43htr evenly spaced down side,

ending just before granny squares, turn. (44 sts)

Row 1: Ch2, miss st at base of ch, 1htr in each st to end, 1htr in top of ch-2, turn. Rep last row 8 times more, ending at edge opposite granny squares.
Fold flap on to WS and work dc join through side of flap and top of A.
Fasten off.

Second Pocket Flap

Attach A to right-hand edge just above granny squares and work second pocket flap as first.
Fasten off after Row 10 and rejoin A at top edge to work dc join.

Finishing

Sew lower side of pocket flaps at end of granny square section using a length of A and yarn needle and working whip st. Each of the yarns is made of several finer strands twisted together. To sew pocket divisions take a 1m (40in) length and untwist it into single strands. Use 2 strands together for seams. Use A, B and C to seam pocket divisions as shown in photograph above, using backstitch – one at centre of each colour section and one at each colour change. Alternatively, you could use embroidery thread in a colour to match the relevant yarn to stitch the pocket divisions.

Attach A to granny square section and edge with dc, working 2 dc in each corner sp.
Fasten off.
Weave in all ends.

Optional: thread ribbon through piece from back to tie.

chunky pointed cowl

Worked with super chunky yarn, this snuggly and beautiful cowl will crochet up in just an evening or two. The sky blue colour will keep you cheerful with thoughts of summer, even in the grey days of winter.

Starting Square

Row 1: Ch3, miss 1 ch, 1dc in each of next 2 ch, turn. (2 sts)

Row 2: Ch1, 2dc in each st, turn. (4 sts)

Row 3: Ch3, 2tr in first st, miss 2 sts, 3tr in last st, turn.

Row 4: Ch3, 2tr in first st, 3tr in sp between tr groups, 3tr in last st, turn.

Row 5: Ch3, 2tr in first st, [3tr in sp between groups] to end, 3tr in last st, turn.

Rep Row 5 eleven times.

Top row: Ch3, 1tr in first st, [3tr in sp between tr groups] to end, 2tr in last st, turn.

With yarn still attached, ss to join ends of Top row together.

Edging

With yarn still attached, ch1, work dc edging around entire lower edge. Fasten off.

Finishing

Weave in ends.

Skill level: Easy

Materials

51% wool/49% acrylic super chunky (bulky) yarn, such as Sirdar Big Softie

* 2 x 50g balls (90m/99yd) in blue
* 10.0mm (US size N/15) crochet hook

Dimensions

* Depth at centre approx 34cm (13½in).
* Exact tension is not important on this project.

Closed granny triangle shawl

Luxuriously worked in a beautifully warm and soft wool, this shawl looks best draped casually around the neck like a huge scarf. You'll find yourself reaching for it on cold evenings and to take a brisk walk in the autumn months.

Skill level: Intermediate

Materials

100% pure wool tweed yarn, such as Rowan Tweed
* 9 x 50g balls (1062m/1161yd) in green
* 5.5mm (US size I/9) crochet hook

Dimensions

* Approx length 110cm (44in); approx width across top edge 150cm (60in).
* Exact tension is not important on this project.

Shawl

Ch4, join with ss in first ch to form a ring.
Rnd 1: Ch3, 2tr in ring, *ch3, 3tr in ring; rep from * once more, ch3, join with ss in top of ch-3.
Rnd 2: Ch3, *1tr in each tr to corner sp, [3tr, ch3, 3tr] in corner sp; rep from * 2 times more, join with ss in top of ch-3.
Rnd 3: Ch3, *1tr in each tr to corner sp, [3tr, ch3, 3tr] in corner sp; rep from * 2 times more, 1tr in each tr to end, join with ss in top of ch-3.
Rep Rnd 3 another 24 times.
Fasten off.

Lace Edging

(worked on 2 sides of triangle)
Row 1: Attach yarn in first tr after any corner sp, ch3, 2tr in same st as join, *miss 3 sts, [3tr, ch2, 3tr] in next st; rep from * along 2 sides of triangle, working [3tr, ch2, 3tr, ch2, 3tr] in sp at corner of first side, ending 3tr in last st before corner sp at end of second side, turn.
Row 2: Ch3, 2tr in st at base of ch, *[3tr, ch2, 3tr] in next ch-2 sp; rep from *, ending 3tr in last st, turn.
Rep last row once more.

Row 4: Ch6, ss in third ch from hook, 2tr in st at base of ch, *[3tr, ch4, ss in third ch from hook, ch1, 3tr] in next ch-2 sp; rep from *, ending 3tr in last st, ch3, ss in same st.
Fasten off.

Finishing

Weave in all ends.

squares iPad and iPhone cover

Marrying the traditional with the hi-tech, these covers are both useful and stunning as well as very fashionable. This is a real stash-busting exercise, as you can use any DK-weight yarn you have lying around.

Skill level: Easy

Materials

* Small amounts of any DK-weight (light worsted) yarn in desired colours, about 1¼ × 50g ball (172m/156yd) of yarn in total
* 4.0mm (US size G/6) crochet hook

Dimensions

* To fit a standard iPad and iPhone size.
* Exact tension is not important on this project.

Notes

A total of 60g of yarn was used for the iPad cover and 15g for the iPhone cover. Back can be worked in stripes if a larger amount of one colour is not available.

iPad Cover Front

(3 squares across and 4 squares down)
Starting square:
Using any colour, ch4, join with ss in first ch to form a ring.
Rnd 1: Ch3, 2tr in ring, *ch2, 3tr in ring; rep from * 2 times more, ch2, join with ss in top of ch-3.
Fasten off.
Rnd 2: Attach new colour in any ch-2 corner sp, ch3, [2tr, ch2, 3tr] in corner sp, *ch1, [3tr, ch2, 3tr] in next corner sp; rep from * 2 times more, ch1, join with ss in top of ch-3.
Fasten off.

Work rem 11 squares as starting square, but use join-as-you-go method (see page 121) on Rnd 2, arranging squares 3 across and 4 down.

Edging

Attach edging colour in any corner sp, ch3, [2tr, ch2, 3tr] in corner sp, *[ch1, 3tr in each ch-1 sp and each join between squares] to corner sp, [3tr, ch2, 3tr] in corner sp; rep from * 2 times more, [ch1, 3tr in each ch-1 sp and each join between squares] to end, ch1, join with ss in top of ch-3.
Fasten off.

iPad Cover Back

Row 1: Using any colour, ch36, miss 2 ch, 1htr in each ch, turn. (34 sts)
Row 2: Ch2, miss first htr, 1htr in each st to end, 1htr in top of 2-ch, turn.
Rep Row 2 another 27 times or until piece measures same as front.
Fasten off.

Finishing

Hold front and back together with WS facing. Attach edging colour to corner of one long edge, ch1, work dc join around 3 sides, working 2dc into both corner ch sps and leaving one short side open.
Fasten off.

iPhone Cover Front

(2 squares)

Starting square:

Using any colour, ch4, join with ss in first ch to form a ring.

Rnd 1: Ch3, 2tr in ring, *ch2, 3tr in ring; rep from * 2 times more, ch2, join with ss in top of ch-3.
Fasten off.

Rnd 2: Attach new colour in any ch-2 corner sp, ch3, [2tr, ch2, 3tr] in corner sp, *ch1, [3tr, ch2, 3tr] in next corner sp; rep from * 2 times more, ch1, join with ss in top of ch-3.
Fasten off.

Work second square as starting square, but use join-as-you-go method (see page 121) on Rnd 2.

Edging

Attach edging colour in any st, ch1, *1dc in each st and ch to corner, 2dc in each corner ch; rep from * 3 times more, 1dc in each st and ch to end, join with ss in first dc.
Fasten off.

iPhone Cover Back

Row 1: Using any colour, ch15, miss 1 ch, 1dc in each ch, turn. (14 sts)

Row 2: Ch1, 1dc in each dc to end, turn. Rep Row 2 another 21 times or until piece measures same as front.
Fasten off.

Finishing

Hold front and back together with WS facing. Attach edging colour to corner of one long edge, ch1, work dc join around 3 sides, working 2dc in each ch at both corners and leaving one short side open.
Fasten off.

granny stripe arm warmers

A beautiful and quick little project, these granny stripe arm warmers are made from luxurious yarns and would be gratefully received as a gift for almost any occasion… but you may not be able to part with them!

Arm Warmers

(make 2)

Row 1: Using A, ch28 very loosely, miss 1ch, 1dc in each rem ch, turn. (27 sts)

Row 2: Ch3, 1tr in same st, *miss 2 sts, 3tr in next st; rep from * to last 2 sts, miss 1 st, 1tr in last st, turn.

Row 3: Attach B, ch3, 2tr in sp before first tr group, 3tr in sp between tr groups across row, ending 2tr in last sp and 1tr in top of ch-3, turn.

Row 4: Ch3, 1tr in sp after first tr, 3tr in each sp between tr groups across row, ending 1tr in top of ch-3, turn.

Change to A.

Rep Rows 3 and 4 another 6 times or to desired length, switching colours after each Row 4.

Work edging:

Using same colour as last row, *miss 1 st, 5htr in next st, miss 1 st, ss in next st; rep from * across row, ending 5tr in top of ch-3.

With yarn still attached, work dc join through both edges down two long sides of square, leaving 5cm (2in) open for thumbhole (work dc into one side but not the other for this opening).

Fasten off.

Re-attach yarn and edge other side of thumbhole with dc.

Fasten off.

Finishing

Weave in all ends.

Skill level: Easy

Materials

100% extra fine merino wool DK (light worsted) yarn, such as Sublime Extra Fine Merino Wool DK

* 1 x 50g ball (approx 116m/127yd) in blue (A)

75% merino/20% silk/5% cashmere DK (light worsted) yarn, such as Sublime Cashmere Merino Silk DK

* 1 x 50g ball (approx 116m/127yd) in pink (B)

* 4.0mm (US size G/6) crochet hook

Dimensions

* Approx length 17cm (6¹⁄₂in).

* Exact tension is not important on this project.

colourful granny stripes scarf

A burst of fresh colour livens up this snuggly scarf. In just a few rows of granny stripes and two edging rounds, you'll have a beautiful accessory to wear or give. A great beginner's project, and a fantastic stash-buster!

Skill level: Easy

Materials

* Approx 400g of any DK-weight (light worsted) yarn in assorted colours
* 4.0mm (US size G/6) crochet hook

Dimensions

* 29 x 160cm (11 1/2 x 63in)
* Exact tension is not important on this project.

Scarf

Row 1: Ch230, miss 1 ch, 1dc in each ch to end, turn.

Row 2: Ch3, 1tr in st at base of ch, *miss 2 sts, 3tr in next st; rep from * to last 3 sts, miss 2 sts, 2tr in last st, turn.

Row 3: Ch3, miss first 2 tr, 3tr in each gap between tr groups to end, 1tr in top of turning ch, turn.

Row 4: Attach new colour, ch3, 1tr in sp before 3-tr group, 3tr in each gap between tr groups to end, ending 1tr in sp after last 3-tr group, 1tr in top of turning ch, turn.

Rep Rows 3 and 4, changing colour every alt row until a total of 12 two-row stripes have been completed, ending with a Row 3.

Edging row 1: Attach first edging colour in any st, ch1, 1dc in same st and each st around entire scarf, working 3dc at each corner, join with ss in first dc. Fasten off.

Edging row 2: Attach second edging colour in any st, ch1, 1dc in same st, *miss 2 sts, [2tr, ch3, ss in 3rd ch from hook, 3tr] in next st, miss 2 sts, 1dc in next st; rep from * around entire scarf, join with ss in first dc. Fasten off.

Finishing

Weave in all ends.

granny square gloves

Challenging to make but fun, these gloves are the ultimate repurposing of granny squares. The fingers can also be worked to only half length to make a pair of fashionable fingerless gloves.

Skill level: Advanced

Materials

100% pure wool DK (light worsted) yarn, such as Rowan Pure Wool DK

* 2 x 50g balls (250m/274yd) in cream (A)

70% acrylic/30% wool DK (light worsted) yarn, such as Sirdar Click DK

* 1 x 50g ball (150m/164yd) in each of green (B) and blue (C)
* 4.0mm (US size G/6) crochet hook

Dimensions

* Each square measures 11cm (4¼in); size around hand 22cm (8½in); length 25cm (10in)
* Exact tension is not important on this project.

Notes

* Gloves are worked WS facing. Weave in all ends on side facing during working.
* Little finger is worked over 8 sts, other 3 fingers are worked over 10 sts. Thumb is worked over 16 sts.
* Work second glove as the first, reversing position of fingers and thumb to make a pair of gloves.

Back of Hand Granny Square

(make 2)
Using B, ch4, join with ss in first ch to form a ring.
Rnd 1: Ch3, 2tr in ring, *ch2, 3tr in ring; rep from * 2 times more, ch2, join with ss in top of ch-3.
Fasten off B.
Rnd 2: Attach A in any ch-2 corner sp, ch3, [2tr, ch2, 3tr] in same sp, *ch1, [3tr, ch2, 3tr] in next corner sp; rep from * 2 times more, ch1, join with ss in top of ch-3.
Fasten off A.
Rnd 3: Attach C in any ch-2 corner sp, ch3, [2tr, ch2, 3tr] in same sp, *ch1, 3tr in next ch-1 sp, ch1, [3tr, ch2, 3tr] in next corner sp; rep from * 2 times more, ch1, 3tr in next ch-1 sp, ch1, join with ss in top of ch-3.
Fasten off C.
Rnd 4: Attach A in any ch-2 corner sp, ch3, [2tr, ch2, 3tr] in same sp, *[ch1, 3tr in next ch-1 sp] 2 times, ch1, [3tr, ch2, 3tr] in next corner sp; rep from * 2 times more, [ch1, 3tr in next ch-1 sp] 2 times, ch1, join with ss in top of ch-3.
Fasten off.

Palm Closed Square

(make 2)
Using A, ch4, join with ss in first ch to form a ring.
Rnd 1: Ch3, 2tr in ring, *ch2, 3tr in ring; rep from * 2 times more, ch2, join with ss in top of ch-3.
Rnd 2: Ch3, *1tr in each st to corner sp, [2tr, ch2, 2tr] in corner sp; rep from * 3 times more, join with ss in top of ch-3.
Rnd 3: Ch3, *1tr in each st to corner sp, [2tr, ch2, 2tr] in corner sp; rep from * 3 times more, 1tr in each rem st, join with ss in top of ch-3.
Rep Rnd 3 once more.
Fasten off.

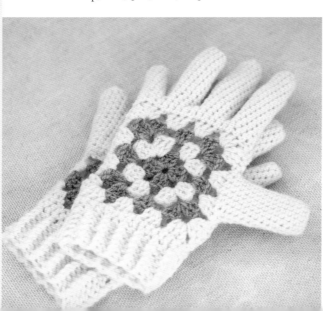

Cuff

Pin one Back of hand granny square and one Palm closed square RS facing. Attach A in first st after any corner sp, ch1, 1dc in same st and each st and ch across one side of square and one side of closed square, join with ss in first dc. (34 sts)

Rnd 1: Ch2, 1htr in each of next 2 sts, hr2tog, *1htr in each of next 3 sts, htr2tog; rep from * to last 4 sts, 1htr in each of next 2 sts, htr2tog, join with ss in top of ch-2. (28 sts)

Rnd 2: Ch2, *fphtr in next st, bphtr in next st; rep from * to end, join with ss in top of ch-2.

Rep Rnd 2 another 5 times.

Fasten off.

Attach A to side of square at top of cuff, ch1, 1dc in same st, work dc join through both squares along side. At top of square, ch1, dc around top of both squares, join with ss in top of first dc. (34 sts)

Fingers

Make little finger:

Rnd 1: Ch1, 1dc in each of next 4 sts, turn, 1dc in equivalent 4 sts on other square, join with ss in first dc.

Rnd 2: Ch1, 1dc in each st, join with ss in first dc.

Rep Rnd 2 until little finger is approx 5cm (2in) long, or try on glove and cont to desired length.

Last rnd: Ch1, dc2tog around, join with ss in first st.

Fasten off, use tail to close rem hole.

Increase rnd: Attach A in st after little finger sts, [1dc in each of next 3 sts, 2dc in next st] around rem finger sts. (30 sts)

Make ring finger:

Leave 20cm (8in) tail when attaching yarn for fingers.

Rnd 1: Ch1, 1dc in each of next 5 sts, turn, 1dc in equivalent 5 sts on other square, join with ss in first dc.

Rnd 2: Ch1, 1dc in each st, join with ss in first dc.

Rep Rnd 2 until ring finger is approx 7cm (2¾in), or try on glove and cont to desired length.

Last rnd: Ch1, dc2tog around, join with ss in first st.

Fasten off, use tail to close rem hole.

Make middle finger:

Attach A in next st after ring finger, work middle finger as ring finger until middle finger is 8cm (3¼in), or try on glove and cont to desired length.

Last rnd: Ch1, dc2tog around, join with ss in first st.

Fasten off, use tail to close rem hole.

Make index finger:

Attach A in next st after middle finger, work index finger as ring finger until index finger is 8cm (3¼in), or try on glove and cont to desired length.

Last rnd: Ch1, dc2tog around, join with ss in first st.

Fasten off, use tail to close rem hole. Join gap at base of fingers with yarn tail.

Make thumb:

Attach A at top of squares below index finger and work dc join through both squares for 2cm (¾in). In uppermost square, 1dc in next 8 sts or ch, turn, 1dc in equivalent 8 sts or ch on other square, join with ss in first dc.

Rnd 1: Ch1, 1dc in each st, join with ss in first dc.

Rep Rnd 1 until thumb is approx 6cm (2½in), or try on glove and cont to desired length.

Last rnd: Ch1, dc2tog around, join with ss in first st.

Fasten off, use tail to close rem hole.

Attach A, ch1, work dc join through both squares from below thumb to top of cuff. Fasten off. Join gap at base of thumb.

Finishing

Weave in all ends.

Turn glove to RS.

granny square gilet

This fashionable gilet is an easy way to enter the world of granny square clothing!
Granny squares are so trendy; they are on the catwalks and in the high-street shops.
Making your own means you can choose yarn you love and customize the fit.

Skill level: Intermediate

Materials

51% wool/49% acrylic chunky (bulky) yarn, such as Sirdar Escape Chunky

* 10 x 50g balls (650m/710yd) in pink/crimson multi
* 6.0mm (US size J/10) crochet hook

Dimensions

* One size fits most.
* Actual size 110cm (43in); length 55cm (21¹/₂in).
* Tension: Each square measures 11cm (4¹/₄in) using 6.0mm (US size J/10) hook, or suitable hook to achieve this.

Notes

* For a slimmer fit, omit rows of three gusset squares at underarms.
* For a larger fit, add another row of gusset squares at centre back.
* For a shorter gilet, work 4 squares long instead of 5.

Basic Square

Ch4, join with ss in first ch to form a ring.

Rnd 1: Ch3, 2tr in ring, *ch2, 3tr in ring; rep from * 2 times more, ch2, join with ss in top of ch-3.

Rnd 2: Ss in each of next 2 tr and first ch of corner sp, ch3, [2tr, ch2, 3tr] in same sp, *ch1, [3tr, ch2, 3tr] in next corner sp; rep from * 2 times more, ch1, join with ss in top of ch-3.

Rnd 3: Ss in each of next 2 tr and first ch of corner sp, ch3, [2tr, ch2, 3tr] in same sp, *ch1, 3tr in next sp, ch1, [3tr, ch2, 3tr] in next corner sp; rep from * 2 times

more, ch1, 3tr in next sp, join with ss in top of ch-3.
Fasten off.

Attach additional squares using join-as-you-go method (see page 121) in Rnd 3 and following chart.

Finishing

Following chart, join two red sections using dc join. Rep for blue sections.

Edging

Attach yarn in any st, ch1, 1dc in same st and in each st and ch around entire gilet, working 2dc in each corner ch at lower corner of fronts.
Edge armholes in dc.
Fasten off.
Weave in all ends.

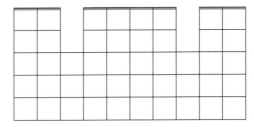

Gilet chart
Two red sections seamed together.
Two blue sections seamed together.

closed granny square **tote**

A surprisingly simple construction gives a functional and attractive shape to this tote bag. The rustic, slubbed texture of the yarn adds visual interest and appeal. Big enough to hold all your daily essentials, you'll reach for this bag again and again!

Squares
(make 12)
Ch4, join with ss in first ch to form a ring.
Rnd 1: Ch3, 2tr in ring, *ch2, 3tr in ring; rep from * 2 times more, ch2, join with ss in top of ch-3.
Rnd 2: Ch3, *1tr in each tr to next corner sp, [2tr, ch2, 2tr] in corner sp; rep from * 3 times more, 1tr in each tr to end, join with ss in top of ch-3.
Rnd 3: Ch3, *1tr in each tr to next corner sp, [2tr, ch2, 2tr] in corner sp; rep from * 3 times more, join with ss in top of ch-3.
Rep Rnd 2 once more.
Fasten off.

Finishing
Assemble using dc join following the chart below. Fold in half diagonally and dc join sides to close, following picture. Weave in all ends.

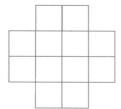

Bag chart
Fold in half diagonally.

Handle
Attach yarn 3 sts away from join of squares on side of open top of bag. Ch1, 1dc in same st and in each of next 2 sts, 1dc in join st, 1dc in each of next 3 sts.
Next row: Ch1, 1dc in each st. (7 sts)
Rep last row 19 times more or to desired length. Ss to equivalent sts on other side of open top of bag, then ss or whip st two long sides of handle together to make it double thickness.
Fasten off.

Skill level: Advanced

Materials

73% viscose/15% silk/12% linen Aran (worsted) yarn, such as Rowan RYC Natural Silk Aran

* 3 x 50g balls (195m/213yd) in pink multi

* 5.0mm (US size H/8) crochet hook

Dimensions

* Each square measures 10cm (4in); width across lower edge 48cm (19in); height to base of handle 20cm (8in).

* Exact tension is not important on this project.

Note

Do not use the join-as-you-go method for this bag. Using solid dc joins instead will add firmness to the structure and prevent holes.

chapter 3

for babies
and children

Mini granny squares and stripes incorporate perfectly into these wee
projects, keeping precious little ones warm and safe. The cot and
pram blankets will be useful and beautiful for years to
come, maybe even wrapping successive generations
of tots in their snuggly folds!

mini granny square bootees

These adorable bootees are the perfect gift for the newborn baby in your life! They work up quickly and can be made in any DK-weight yarn. I chose lavender and cream so they would suit either a boy or a girl.

Skill level: Intermediate

Materials

55% merino/33% microfibre/12% cashmere DK (light worsted) yarn, such as Debbie Bliss Cashmerino DK

* 1 x 50g ball (approx 110m/120yd) each in lavender (A) and cream (B)
* 4.0mm (US size G/6) crochet hook

Dimensions

* Length 10cm (4in), will fit most newborns.
* Tension: 20 sts to 10cm (4in) working in dc using 4.00mm (US size G/6) hook, or suitable hook to achieve this.

Note:

Top of bootee and sole are worked separately and then joined. Sole is worked with WS facing.

Top

Using A, ch4, join with ss to form a ring.
Rnd 1: Ch2, 2htr in ring, *ch2, 3htr in ring; rep from * 2 times more, ch2, join with ss in top of ch-2.
Fasten off A.
Rnd 2: Join B in any ch-2 sp, ch2, [2htr, ch2, 3htr] all in same sp, *ch1, [3htr, ch2, 3htr] in next corner sp; rep from * 2 times more, ch1, join with ss in top of ch-2.
Fasten off B.
Rnd 3: Join A in any ch-2 corner sp, ch2, 1htr in same sp, *1htr in each st and ch across next side of square, 2htr in corner sp; rep from * once more, 1htr in each st and ch across next side of square, [2htr, ch2, 2htr] in corner sp, 1htr in each st and ch across last side of square, [2htr, ch2] in original corner sp, join with ss in top of ch-2.
Form toe:
Begin to work back and forth in rows around 3 sides of square.
Row 1: Ch2, *1htr in each st of next side, htr2tog using 2 corner sts; rep from * once more, 1htr in each st of next side. Leave last side unworked, turn.
Row 2: Rep Row 1 once more.
Fasten off.

Sole

Work in the rnd throughout sole, use stitch marker to mark first st of rnd.
Using A, ch9.
Rnd 1: Miss first ch, 4dc in next ch, 1dc in next 6 chs, 4dc in last ch. Working down other side of ch, 1dc in each of next 6 chs, join with ss in first dc.
Rnd 2: *2dc in each of next 4 sts, 1dc in next 6 sts; rep from * once more, join with ss in first dc.
Rnd 3: *[1dc in next st, 2dc in next st] 4 times, 1dc in next 6 sts; rep from * once more, join with ss in first dc.
Rnd 4: *[1dc in each of next 2 sts, 2dc in next st] 4 times, 1dc in next 6 sts; rep from * once more, join with ss in first dc.
Rnd 5: 1dc in each st.
Form heel:
Begin to work back and forth in rows.
Row 1: Ch2, 1htr in next 14 sts, turn.
Row 2: Rep Row 1.
Fasten off A.
Row 3: Join B, ch2, 1htr in next 14 sts.
Fasten off.

Finishing

Sew sole and toe sections together using whip st and a yarn needle. Sew row-ends of heel to row-ends of toe section.
Weave in all ends.

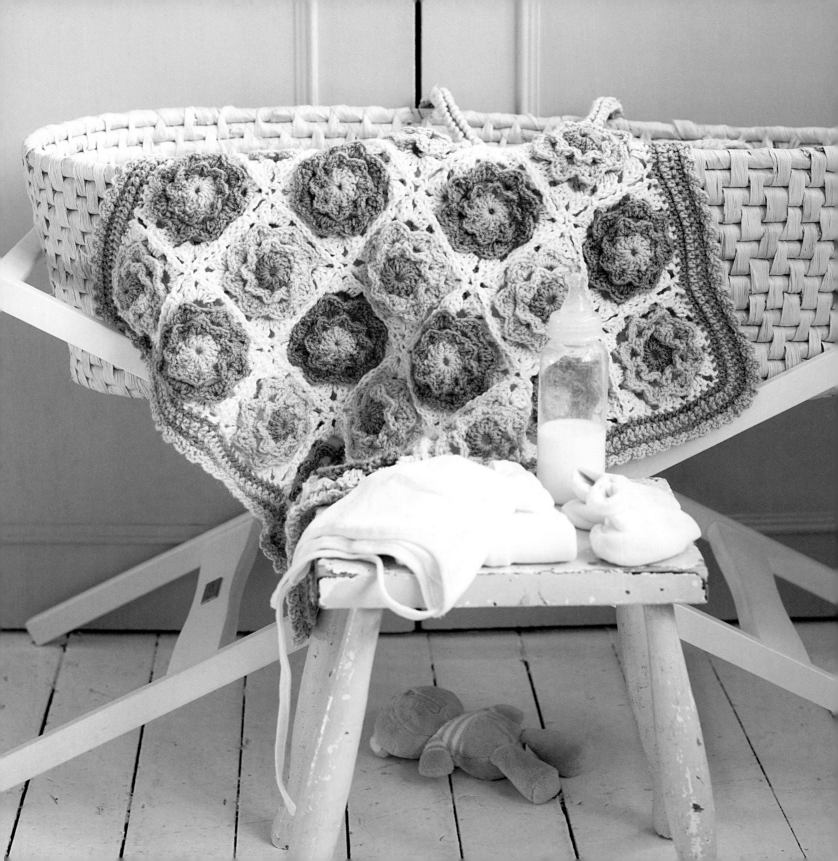

sweet posies **pram blanket**

A perfect gift for a baby shower, birth celebration or christening, this lovely blanket is just the right size for a pram or stroller – big enough to keep baby snuggly warm, but not so big it will drag on the ground. If desired, additional squares can be added to make a full-size cot or bed blanket.

Posy Square

Using A or B, ch4, join with ss in first ch to form a ring.

Rnd 1: Ch3, 15tr in ring, join with ss in top of ch-3.

Fasten off.

Rnd 2: Attach B or A in any st, ch1, *[1dc, 1htr, 1tr, 1htr, 1dc] in same st, miss next st; rep from * around, join with ss in first dc. (8 petals)

Rnd 3: Ch1, working behind petals, *BPSS (see page 123) round post of tr at centre of next petal, ch3; rep from * around, join with ss in ch-1.

Rnd 4: Ss into first ch-3 sp, ch1, *[1dc, 1htr, 3tr, 1htr, 1dc] in next sp; rep from * around, join with ss in first dc.

Rnd 5: Ch1, working behind petals, *BPSS round post of centre tr of next petal, ch 5; rep from * around, join with ss in ch-1.

Fasten off.

Rnd 6: Attach C in any ch-5 sp, ch3, [2tr, ch2, 3tr] in same sp, *ch1, 3tr in next ch-5 sp, ch1, [3tr, ch2, 3tr] in next ch-5 sp; rep from * 2 times more, ch1, 3tr in last ch-5 sp, ch1, join with ss in top of ch-3.

Fasten off.

Make another 24 squares, using the join-as-you-go method (see page 121) in Rnd 6, reversing use of A and B for each square. Arrange squares in 5 rows of 5.

Edging

Rnd 1: Attach B in any st, ch2, 1htr in each st around entire blanket, working 2htr in each of 2 sts at corners, join with ss in top of ch-2.

Rnd 2: Rep Rnd 1 using A.

Rnd 3: Rep Rnd 1 using B.

Picot rnd: Attach A in any st, ch 1, [1dc, ch3, 1dc] in same st, *miss next st, [1dc, ch3, 1dc] in next st; rep from * around entire blanket, eliminating 2 missed sts at each corner.

Finishing

Weave in all ends.

Skill level: Intermediate

Materials

70% acrylic/30% wool DK (light worsted) yarn, such as Sirdar Click DK

* 3 × 50g balls (450m/492yd) in pink (A)

* 2 × 50g balls (300m/328yd) in blue (B)

100% acrylic Aran (worsted) yarn, such as Sirdar Supersoft Aran

* 1 × 100g ball (approx 236m/258yd) in white multi (C)

* 4.5mm (US size 7) crochet hook

Dimensions

* Each square measures 10cm (4in); finished blanket measures 58cm (22³/₄in) square.

* Exact tension is not important on this project.

mini square detail baby hat

A mini granny square detail strip livens up this sweet pull on hat for a baby. Worked in rounds after the granny squares are completed, this adorable accessory is finished in a flash and would be an ideal last-minute gift.

Starting Square

Using A, ch4, ss in first ch to form a ring.
Rnd 1: Ch3, 2tr in centre of ring, *ch2, 3tr in centre of ring; rep from * 2 times more, ch2, join with ss in top of ch-3.
Rnd 2: Attach B in any ch-2 corner sp, ch3, [2tr, ch2, 3tr] all in same corner sp, *ch1, [3tr, ch2, 3tr] in next corner sp; rep from * 2 times more, ch1, join with ss in top of ch-3.
Rnd 3: Attach A in any ch-2 corner sp, ch3, [2tr, ch2, 3tr] all in same corner sp, *ch1, 3tr in next sp, ch1, [3tr, ch2, 3 tr] in next corner sp; rep from * 2 times more, ch1, 3tr in next sp, ch1, join with ss in top of ch-3.
Fasten off.

Make 3 more squares using the join-as-you-go method (see page 121) in Rnd 3. Seam ends of last and first squares together with ss join to make a ring.

Hat

Working along top edge of ring, attach A in any st.
Rnd 1: Make 50 dc evenly spaced around. Work in continuous rnds.
Rnd 2: [8dc, dc2tog] 5 times. (45 sts)
Rnd 3: [7dc, dc2tog] 5 times. (40 sts)
Rnd 4: [6dc, dc2tog] 5 times. (35 sts)
Rnd 5: [5dc, dc2tog] 5 times. (30 sts)
Rnd 6: [4dc, dc2tog] 5 times. (25 sts)
Rnd 7: [3dc, dc2tog] 5 times. (20 sts)
Rnd 8: [2dc, dc2tog] 5 times. (15 sts)
Rnd 9: [1dc, dc2tog] 5 times. (10 sts)
Cut yarn, leaving a long tail. Weave tail through rem sts then draw closed like a drawstring and fasten off securely.

Edging

Working on bottom edge of square ring, attach A in any st.
Rnd 1: Ch2, work 55htr evenly around ring, join with ss in top of ch-2 to close.
Rnds 2–3: Ch2, *working around post of st in rnd below, fphtr (see page 123) in next st, bphtr in next st; rep from * to last st, fphtr in last st, join with ss in top of ch-2.
Fasten off.

Finishing

Weave in all ends.

Skill level: Intermediate

Materials

55% merino/33% microfibre/12% cashmere baby (fingering/sport) yarn, such as Debbie Bliss Baby Cashmerino

* 1 x 50g ball (approx 125m/137yd) in bright blue (A)

  Small amount of cream (B)

* 3.5mm (US size E/4) crochet hook

Dimensions

* To fit newborn to 3 months.

* Exact tension is not important on this project.

squares and stripes cardigan

You'll be surprised how easily this adorable cardigan works up. Featuring squares at the bottom and sleeve edges and lively stripes throughout, this fantastic little garment will keep your favourite babe snuggly warm.

Skill level: Intermediate

Materials

75% merino/20% silk/5% cashmere lightweight Aran (light worsted) yarn, such as Sublime Cashmere Merino Silk Aran

∗ 2 x 50g balls (approx 172m/188yd) in mauve (A)

100% pure wool DK (light worsted) yarn, such as Rowan Pure Wool DK

∗ 2 x 50g balls (250m/274yd) in cream (B)

∗ 5.0mm (US size H/8) crochet hook

∗ 2cm (³/₄in) button

Dimensions

∗ To fit newborn to 3 months.

∗ Tension: 13 sts and 11 rows to 10cm (4in) working in htr using 5.0mm (US size H/8) hook, or suitable hook to achieve this.

Starting Square

Using B, ch4, join with ss in first ch to form a ring.

Rnd 1: Ch3, 2tr in ring, *ch2, 3tr in ring; rep from * 2 times more, ch2, join with ss in top of ch-3.

Rnd 2: Attach A in any corner sp, ch3, [2tr, ch2, 3tr] all in same sp, *ch1, [3tr, ch2, 3tr] in next corner sp; rep from * 2 times more, ch1, join with ss in top of ch-3.

Rnd 3: Attach B in any corner sp, ch3, [2tr, ch2, 3tr] all in same sp, *ch1, 3tr in next sp, ch1, [3tr, ch2, 3tr] in next corner sp; rep from * 2 times more, ch1, 3tr in next sp, ch1, join with ss in top of ch-3.

Make 4 more squares, working Rnds 1 and 2 the same but using the join-as-you-go method (see page 121) on Rnd 3 to make a strip of 5 squares.

Cardigan

Begin to work back and forth in rows.

Row 1: Attach A at end of long side of strip, ch2, work 63 htr evenly across long side of strip. (64 sts)

Row 2: Attach B in top of first ch from prev row, ch2, miss st at base of ch-2, work htr across row ending 1htr in top of ch-2, turn.

At start of every row miss st at base of ch-2 and at end work into top of ch-2.

Row 3: Ch2, 1htr in each st to end, turn.

Row 4: Using A, ch2, 1htr in each st to end, turn.

Row 5: Ch2, 1htr in each st to end, turn.

Rep Rows 2 and 3 once more, then divide for fronts and back.

First Front

Row 1: Using A, ch2, htr2tog, 1htr in each of next 13 sts, turn. (15 sts)

Row 2: Ch2, 1htr in each st across, ending htr2tog, turn. (14 sts)

Row 3: Using B, ch2, htr2tog, 1htr in each st to end, turn. (13 sts)

Row 4: Ch2, 1htr in each st across, ending htr2tog, turn. (12 sts)

Row 5: Using A, ch2, htr2tog, 1htr in each st to end, turn. (11 sts)

Rep Rows 2–4 once more. (8 sts)

Row 9: Using A, ch2, 1htr in each st to end, turn.

Row 10: Rep Row 9. Fasten off.

Back

Row 1: Attach A in next st after first front sts, ch2, 1htr in each of next 31 sts, turn. (32 sts)

Row 2: Ch2, 1htr in each st to end, turn.

Row 3: Using B, ch2, 1htr in each st to end, turn.

Row 4: Ch2, 1htr in each st to end, turn.

Row 5: Using A, ch2, 1htr in each st to end, turn. (11 sts)

Rep Rows 2–5 once more and then Row 2 once more. Fasten off.

Second Front

Row 1: Attach A in next st after back sts, ch2, 1htr in each st, ending htr2tog, turn. (15 sts)

Row 2: Ch2, htr2tog, 1htr in each st to end, turn. (14 sts)

Row 3: Using B, ch1, 1htr in each st, ending htr2tog, turn. (13 sts)

Row 4: Ch2, htr2tog, htr in each st to end, turn. (12 sts)

Row 5: Using A, ch2, 1htr in each st, ending htr2tog, turn. (11 sts)

Rep Rows 2–5 once more. (8 sts)

Row 9: Using A, ch2, 1htr in each st to end, turn.

Row 10: Rep Row 9. Fasten off.

Sleeves
(make 2)

Starting square:

Using B, ch4, join with ss in first ch to form a ring.

Rnd 1: Ch3, 2tr in ring, *ch2, 3tr in ring; rep from * 2 times more, ch2, join with ss in top of ch-3.

Rnd 2: Attach A in any corner sp, ch3, [2tr, ch2, 3tr] all in same sp, *ch1, [3tr, ch2, 3tr] in next corner sp; rep from * 2 times more, ch1, join with ss in top of ch-3.

For second sleeve square, work Rnd 1 as Starting square, but use join-as-you-go method (see page 121) on Rnd 2 to make 2 joined squares. Begin to work back and forth in rows.

Row 1: Attach B at end of long side of strip, ch2, work 21 htr evenly across long side of strip, turn. (22 sts)

Row 2: Ch2, 1htr in st at base of ch-2, 1htr in each st to end, turn. (23 sts)

Row 3: Using A, ch2, 1htr in st at base of ch-2, 1htr in each st to end, turn. (24 sts)

Row 4: Ch2, 1htr in st at base of ch-2, 1htr in each st to end, turn. (25 sts)

Row 5: Using B, ch2, 1htr in st at base of ch-2, 1htr in each st to end, turn. (26 sts)

Rep Rows 2–5 once and then Row 2 once more. (31 sts) Fasten off.

Finishing

Join shoulder seams. Attach A in any st at back neck, ch1, work dc edging around entire body, working a 4-ch buttonhole at bottom of v-neck.

Join sleeve seams using mattress st. Sew on sleeves.

Weave in all ends.

Attach button to other front to match up with buttonhole.

flower square bib

A corsage of sweet white flowers borders the base of this useful and pretty bib. Made with washable yarns for easy care, this is a fabulous baby shower gift that will certainly be well used for some time to come.

Skill level: Advanced

Materials

50% organic wool/50% cotton DK (light worsted) yarn, such as Rowan Belle Organic DK

* 1 x 50g ball (120m/131yd) in blue (A)

100% cotton DK (light worsted) yarn, such as Debbie Bliss Cotton DK

* 1/2 x 50g ball (42m/46yd) in white (B)
* 4.0mm (US size G/6) crochet hook
* 1cm (1/2in) button

Dimensions

* Length from front neck to bottom edge 18cm (7³/4in); width approx 23cm (9¹/4in).
* Exact tension is not important on this project.

Starting Square

Using B, ch4, join with ss in first ch to form a ring.

Rnd 1: *Ch2, 2tr in ring, ch2, ss in ring; rep from * 3 times more.

Rnd 2: *Ch3, working behind petals, ss between petals; rep from * 3 times more.

Rnd 3: Working behind petals, *ss in next ch-3 sp, [ch2, 3tr, ch2, ss] in same sp; rep from * 3 times more.

Rnd 4: *Ch4, working behind petals, ss between petals; rep from * 3 times more.

Rnd 5: Working behind petals, ss in first ch-4 sp, ch3, [2tr, ch2, 3tr] in same sp, *ch1, [3tr, ch2, 3tr] in next ch-4 sp; rep

from * 2 times more, ch1, join with ss in top of first ch-3.
Fasten off.

Work 3 more squares as Starting square, but use the join-as-you-go method (see page 121) in Rnd 5.

Bib

Attach A in corner sp at beg of short side of rectangle, ch1, 1dc in each st and ch around 3 sides of rectangle, 2dc in bottom two corner sps. When 3 sides are completed, ch2, 1htr in each st and ch across rem long side, join with ss in first dc.

Begin working back and forth in rows.

Row 1: Ch2, 1htr in each st across, turn. (36 sts)

Rep Row 1 until piece measures 17cm (6³/4in) from bottom edge.

First side:

Row 1: Ch2, 1htr in each of next 11 sts, turn. Work on these sts only.

Row 2: Ch2, htr2tog, 1htr in each rem st, turn. (11 sts)

Row 3: Ch2, 1htr in each st to end, turn.

Row 4: Ch2, htr2tog, 1htr in each rem st, turn. (10 sts)

Row 5: Ch2, 1htr in each st to end, turn.

Row 6: Ch2, htr2tog, 1htr in each rem st, turn. (9 sts)

Row 7: Ch2, 1htr in each st to end, turn.

Row 8: Ch2, htr2tog, 1htr in each rem st, turn. (8 sts)

Row 9: Ch2, 1htr in each st to end, turn.

Row 10: Ch2, htr2tog, 1htr in each rem st, turn. (7 sts)

Row 11: Ch2, 1htr in each st to end, turn.

Row 12: Ch2, htr2tog, 1htr in each of next 2 sts, htr2tog, turn. (5 sts)

Row 13: Ch1, 1dc in each st to end, turn. Rep Row 13 another 5 times. (6 plain rows total)

Row 19: Ch1, 1dc in each of next 2 sts, ch1, miss 1 dc, 1dc in each of last 2 sts. (buttonhole made)

Fasten off.

Second side:

Miss centre 12 sts, rejoin yarn to next st and work Rows 1–18 to match first side but work each htr2tog at opposite end of row to reverse neck shaping.

Work 1 more row in dc.

Fasten off.

Edging

Attach B in any st and work dc edging around entire piece.

Fasten off.

Finishing

Weave in all ends. Sew button on opposite side of neck to buttonhole.

granny stripe elf hat

Capable of melting anyone's heart, especially a new mum, this playful hat has a granny stripe feature detail around the base and a big fluffy pompom to top it all off. It will certainly keep any baby warm and looking cute!

Skill level: Advanced

Materials

70% acrylic/30% wool DK (light worsted) yarn, such as Sirdar Click DK

* I x 50g ball (150m/164yd) in blue (A)

100% pure wool DK (light worsted) yarn, such as Rowan Pure Wool DK

* I x 50g ball (125m/137yd) in cream (B)

* 4.0mm (US size G/6) crochet hook

Dimensions

* To fit newborn to 3 months.

* Tension: 15htr to 10cm (4in) using 4.00mm (US size G/6) crochet hook, or suitable hook to achieve this.

Hat

Using B, ch2, 9htr in 2nd ch from hook, using A, join with ss in top of ch-2. (10 sts)

Rnd 2: Using A, ch2, 1htr in each st, using B, join with ss in top of ch-2. (10 sts)

Rnd 3: Using B, ch2, 2htr in next st, *1htr in next st, 2htr in next st; rep from * to end, using A, join with ss in top of ch-2. (18 sts)

Rnd 4: Using A, ch2, 1htr in each st, using B, join with ss in top of ch-2. (18 sts)

Rnd 5: Using B, ch2, 1htr in next st, 2htr in next st, *1htr in each of next 2 sts, 2htr in next st; rep from * to end, using A, join with ss in top of ch-2. (24 sts)

Rnd 6: Using A, ch2, 1htr in each st, using B, join with ss in top of ch-2. (24 sts)

Rnd 7: Using B, ch2, 1htr in each of next 2 sts, 2htr in next st, *1htr in each of next 3 sts, 2htr in next st; rep from * to end, using A, join with ss in top of ch-2. (30 sts)

Rnd 8: Using A, ch2, 1htr in each st, using B, join with ss in top of ch-2. (30 sts)

Rep last rnd 5 times more, changing colour every rnd. (6 straight rnds total)

Rnd 14: Using A, ch2, 1htr in each of next 3 sts, 2htr in next st, *1htr in each of next 4 sts, 2htr in next st; rep from * to end, using B, join with ss in top of ch-2. (36 sts)

Rnd 15: Using B, ch2, 1htr in each st, using A, join with ss in top of ch-2. (36 sts)

Rep last rnd 5 times more, changing colour every rnd. (6 straight rnds total)

Rnd 21: Using B, ch2, 1htr in each of next 4 sts, 2htr in next st, *1htr in each of next 5 sts, 2htr in next st; rep from * to end, using A, join with ss in top of ch-2. (42 sts)

Rnd 22: Using A, ch2, 1htr in each st, using B, join with ss in top of ch-2. (42 sts)

Rep last rnd 5 times more, changing colour every rnd. (6 straight rnds total)

Rnd 28: Using A, ch2, 1htr in each of next 4 sts, 2htr in next st, *1htr in each of next 5 sts, 2htr in next st; rep from * to end, using B, join with ss in top of ch-2. (49 sts)

Rnd 29: Using B, ch2, 1htr in each of next 5 sts, 2htr in next st, *1htr in each of next 6 sts, 2htr in next st; rep from * to end, using A, join with ss in top of ch-2. (56 sts)

Rnd 30: Using A, ch2, 1htr in each of next 6 sts, 2htr in next st, *1htr in each of next 7 sts, 2htr in next st; rep from * to end, using B, join with ss in top of ch-2. (63 sts)

Rnd 31: Using B, ch3, 2tr in same st as join, *miss 2 sts, 3tr in next st; rep from * to end, using same colour (B), ss in top of ch-3 to join.

Rnd 32: Using B, ss to first sp between tr groups, using A, ss into sp, ch3, 2tr in same sp, *3tr in next sp between tr groups; rep from * to end, using B, join with ss in top of ch-3.

Rnd 33: Using B, ch2, 1htr in each st, using B, join with ss in top of ch-2. (63 sts)

Rnd 34: Using B, ch2, *working around posts of htr, fphtr (see page 123) in next st, bphtr in next st; rep from * to end, using B, join with ss in top of ch-2.

Rep last rnd once more.

Fasten off.

Finishing

Sew in ends. Make pompom and attach to top of hat.

Pompom

Cut two circles of stiff card the same diameter as the pompom is to be, then cut out a circle from the centre of each that measures half the diameter of the larger circle. Place the two card rings together and wind a doubled length of A through the hole in the centre and then around the edge of the card ring, repeating until the centre hole is packed fairly full of yarn. Cut a separate 30cm (12in) length of yarn and set aside. Slide the tip of a pair of scissors between the two card rings and cut through the yarn all around the edge. Slide the separate piece of yarn between the two card rings, wrap tightly around the centre of the pompom and knot firmly in place. Remove the card rings, fluff up the pompom and trim any uneven ends, leaving one tie end long to sew the pompom onto the hat.

sparkly flower **headband**

A beautiful accessory for a very special baby girl, this gorgeous headband uses the flowers
from the flower square bib on page 92, but is made in a lovely sparkly
yarn and three pretty, soft colours.

Skill level: Intermediate

Materials

53% nylon/43% acrylic/4% polyester
DK (light worsted) yarn, such as Sirdar
Snuggly Pearls DK

* Small amount of white (A) and
pale pink (B)

55% nylon/45% acrylic DK (light
worsted) yarn, such as Wendy Peter
Pan DK

* Small amount of pink (C)
* 4.0mm (US size G/6) crochet hook
* Button

Dimensions

* Each square measures 5.5cm (2¼in);
headband measures 35 x 6cm
(13¾ x 6¼in).

* Exact tension is not important on
this project.

Starting Square
Using A, ch4, join with ss in first ch to
form a ring.
Rnd 1: *Ch2, 2tr in ring, ch2, ss in ring;
rep from * 3 times more.
Rnd 2: *Ch3, working behind petals, ss
between petals; rep from * 3 times more.
Fasten off.
Rnd 3: Using B and working behind
petals, *ss in next ch-3 sp, [ch2, 3tr, ch2,
ss] in same sp; rep from * 3 times more.
Rnd 4: *Ch4, working behind petals, ss
between petals; rep from * 3 times more.
Fasten off.
Rnd 5: Using C and working behind
petals, ss in first ch-4 sp, ch3, [2tr, ch2,
3tr] in same sp, *ch1, [3tr, ch2, 3tr] in
next ch-4 sp; rep from * 2 times more,
ch1, join with ss in top of ch-3.
Fasten off.

Work another 5 squares as Starting
square, but use the join-as-you-go
method (see page 121) in Rnd 5.

Finishing
Using A, work dc edging evenly around
entire piece, working a 6-ch button loop
in the centre of one short side. Attach
button securely to other short side.
Weave in all ends.

dot in a square cot blanket

Simple squares with fabulously puffy and smooshy circle centres are made in soft colours to form this appealing cot blanket. A ruffled edge adds a pretty touch. Squares can efficiently be worked 'assembly line' style if desired, making all the centres first, all the contrasting rounds next, then joined with the join-as-you-go method for the final round.

Skill level: Intermediate

Materials

100% pure wool DK (light worsted) yarn, such as Rowan Pure Wool DK

* 5 x 50g balls (625m/685yd) in cream (A)

* 2 x 50g balls (250m/274yd) in pink (B)

70% acrylic/30% wool DK (light worsted) yarn, such as Sirdar Click DK

* 2 x 50g balls (300m/328yd) in each of blue (C) and green (D)

* 4.5mm (US size 7) crochet hook

Dimensions

* Cot blanket was made with 6 rows, each of 7 squares; each square measures 10cm (4in). Additional squares can be added for a larger blanket. Finished blanket measures 73 x 63cm (28³/₄ x 24³/₄in) including ruffled edging.

* Exact tension is not important on this project.

Squares

(make 42)
Using first colour, ch5, join with ss in first ch to form a ring.

Rnd 1: Ch1, 12dc in ring, ss to first dc to join.

Rnd 2: Working over top of sts from Rnd 1, ch1, 16htr in centre of ring spreading stitches evenly, ss to first htr to join.

Rnd 3: Working over top of sts from Rnd 2, ch1, 24tr in centre of ring spreading sts evenly, ss to first tr to join.
Fasten off first colour. (Centre made)

Rnd 4: Join second colour in any st, ch3, 1tr in same st, [2htr in next st, 2dc in each of next 2 sts, 2htr in next st, 2tr in

next st, ch2, 2tr in next st] 3 times, 2htr in next st, 2dc in each of next 2 sts, 2htr in last st, 2tr in next st, ch2, join with ss in top of ch-3.
Fasten off.

Joining Round

(complete one square first)

Rnd 5: Attach A in any ch-2 corner sp, ch3, [2tr, ch2, 3tr] in same sp as join, [ch1, miss 2 sts, 3tr in next st] 3 times, *ch1, [3tr, ch2, 3tr] in ch-2 corner sp, [ch1, miss 2 sts, 3tr in next st] 3 times; rep from * 2 times more, ch1, join with ss in top of ch-3.
Fasten off.

Finishing

Attach each additional square when working Rnd 5 using join-as-you-go method (see page 121) to give 6 rows each of 7 squares. If preferred, all squares can be completed with Rnd 5 without join-as-you-go, then seamed together with ss or dc join. Weave in all ends.

Edging

Using A, attach in any st, ch3, 1tr in same st, 2tr in every st and ch around entire blanket, working 2tr in each of 2 chs at corners, join with ss in top of ch-3.

Row 5: Ch1, 1dc in each of next 16 sts, ch1, TWOFR (see page 123), 1dc in each of next 13 sts, ch1, TWOFR, 1dc in each of next 12 sts, ch1, TWOFR, 1dc in each of next 11 sts, ch1, TWOFR, 1dc in each of next 10 sts, ch1, TWOFR, 1dc in each of next 9 sts, ch1, TWOFR, 1dc in each of next 9 sts, and 1dc in each of 1 + 1+ 2 sts from lower in row, turn.

Row 6: Ch1, 1dc in each of next 13 sts and 1dc in each of 1 + 1 + 3 sts from lower in row, turn. (18 sts)

Row 7: Ch1, 1dc in each of next 5 sts, dc2tog, 1dc in each of next 4 sts, dc2tog, 1dc in each of next 5 sts, turn. (16 sts)

Row 8: Ch1, 1dc in each st, turn. (16 sts)

Row 9: Ch1, [1dc in next st, dc2tog] 2 times, 1dc in each of next 4 sts, [dc2tog, 1dc in next st] 2 times, turn. (12 sts)

Row 10: Ch1, 1dc in each st, turn. (12 sts)

Row 11: Ch1, 1dc in each of next 2 sts, dc2tog, 1dc in each of next 4 sts, dc2tog, 1dc in next 2 sts, turn. (10 sts)

Row 12: Ch1, 1dc in each of 10 sts, do not turn, ch10 for first arm.

Row 13: Miss 1 ch, 1dc in each of next 9 ch, 1dc in each of 10 body sts, then ch10 for second arm, turn.

Row 14: Miss 1 ch, 1dc in each of next 9 ch, 1dc in each of 19 sts, turn. (28 sts)

Rows 15–18: Ch1, 1dc in each st, turn. (28 sts)

Back of Head

Row 1: Ch1, 1dc in each of next 19 sts, TWOFR.

Row 2: Ch1, dc2tog, 1dc in each of next 6 sts, dc2tog, TWOFR. (8 sts)

Row 3: Ch1, 1dc in each of next 8 sts, turn. (8 sts)

Row 4: Ch1, 2dc in next st, 1dc in next st, 2dc in next st, 1dc in each of next 2 sts, 2dc in next st, 1dc in next st, 2dc in next st, turn. (12 sts)

Row 5: Ch1, 1dc in each st, turn. (12 sts)

Row 6: Ch1, 2dc in next st, 1dc in each of next 3 sts, 2dc in next st, 1dc in each of next 2 sts, 2dc in next st, 1dc in each of next 3 sts, ch1, TWOFR, 1dc in each of next 11 sts, ch1, TWOFR, 1dc in each of next 10 sts, ch1, TWOFR, 1dc in each of next 9 sts, ch1, TWOFR, 1dc in each of next 8 sts, 1dc in each of 1 + 1 sts and 2dc in last st from lower in row, turn.

Row 7: Ch1, 1dc in each of 12 sts and 1dc in each of 1 + 3 sts from lower in row, turn. (16 sts)

Row 8: Ch1, 2dc in next st, 1dc in each of next 3 sts, 2dc in next st, 1dc in each of next 6 sts, 2dc in next st, 1dc in each of next 3 sts, 2dc in next st, turn. (20 sts)

Row 9: Ch1, 1dc in each st, turn. (20 sts)

Row 10: Ch1, 1dc in each of next 4 sts, 2dc in next st, 1dc in each of next 10 sts, 2dc in next st, 1dc in each of next 4 sts, turn. (22 sts)

Row 11: Ch1, 1dc in each st, turn. (22 sts)

Row 12: Ch1, 1dc in each of next 5 sts, dc2tog, 1dc in each of next 8 sts, dc2tog, 1dc in each of next 5 sts, turn. (20 sts)

Row 13: Ch1, 1dc in each st, turn. (20 sts)

Row 14: Ch1, 1dc in each of next 2 sts, dc2tog, [1dc in each of next 5 sts, dc2tog] 2 times, 1dc in each of next 2 sts, turn. (17 sts)

Row 15: Ch1, 1dc in each st, turn. (17 sts)

Row 16: Ch1, 1dc in each of next 15 sts, ch1, TWOFR, 1dc in each of next 13 sts, ch1, TWOFR, 1dc in each of next 11 sts, ch1, TWOFR, 1dc in each of next 9 sts, ch1, TWOFR, 1dc in each of next 7 sts, ch1, TWOFR, 1dc in each of next 5 sts, ch1, TWOFR, 1dc in each of next 5 sts, 1dc in each of 2 + 2 sts and dc2tog over last 2 sts from lower in row, turn.

Row 17: Ch1, 1dc in each of next 10 sts, 1dc in each of 2 + 2 sts and dc2tog over last 2 sts from lower in row, turn. (15 sts)

First ear:

Row 1: Ch1, 1dc in each of next 5 sts, TWOFR. (5 sts)

Row 2: Ch1 1dc in each st, turn. (5 sts)

Row 3: Ch1, [2dc in next st, 1dc in next st] 2 times, 2dc in next st, turn. (8 sts)

Rows 4–5: Ch1, 1dc in each st, turn. (8 sts)

Row 6: Ch1, dc2tog, 1dc in each of next 4 sts, dc2tog, turn. (6 sts)

Row 7: Ch1, dc2tog, 1dc in each of next 2 sts, dc2tog, turn. (4 sts)

Row 8: Ch1, (dc2tog) 2 times. (2 sts)

Fasten off.

Second ear:

Attach A at other end of head, ch1, 1dc in next 5 sts, leaving 5 sts between ears. Work as other ear from Row 2.

Mini Granny Paws

(make 4)

Using B and 4.0mm (US size G/6) hook, ch4, join with ss to form a ring.

Rnd 1: Ch2, 2htr in ring, *ch2, 3htr in ring; rep from * 2 times more, ch2, join with ss in top of ch-2.

Fasten off.

Rnd 2: Join C in any corner sp, ch2,

[2htr, ch2, 3htr] all in same sp, *ch1, [3htr, ch2, 3htr] in next corner sp; rep from * 2 times more, ch1, join with ss in top of ch-2.

Fasten off.

Front of First Leg

Row 1: Attach A to one side of mini granny square. Using 6.0mm (US size J/10) hook, ch1, dc 8 sts evenly across one side, turn. (8 sts)

Row 2: Ch1, 1dc in each st, turn. (8 sts)

Rows 3–7: Rep last row.

Row 8: Ch1, 1dc in next st, dc2tog, 1dc in each of next 2 sts, dc2tog, 1dc in next st. (6 sts)

Fasten off.

Work Second leg as First leg, but do not fasten off.

Joining row: Ch1, 1dc in each of 6 sts of Second leg, ch1, 1dc in 6 sts of First leg, turn. (13 sts incl ch at centre)

Body

Row 1: Ch1, 1dc in each of next 5 sts, 2dc in next st, 1dc in next st, 2dc in next st, 1dc in each of next 5 sts, turn. (15 sts)

Row 2: Ch1, 1dc in each st, turn. (15 sts)

Row 3: Ch1, 2dc in next st, 1dc in next 5 sts, 2dc in next st, 1dc in next st, 2dc in next st, 1dc in each of next 5 sts, 2dc in next st, turn. (19 sts)

Row 4: Ch1, 1dc in each st, turn. (19 sts)

Row 5: Ch1, 1dc in each of next 15 sts, ch1, TWOFR, 1dc in each of next 10 sts, ch1, TWOFR, 1dc in each of next 8 sts, ch1, TWOFR, 1dc in each of next 6 sts, ch1, TWOFR, 1dc in each of next 4 sts, ch1, TWOFR, 1dc in each of next 2 sts, ch1, TWOFR, 1dc in each of next 2 sts and 1dc in each of 2 + 2 + 4 sts from lower in row, turn.

Row 6: Ch1, 1dc in each of 10 sts and 1dc in each of 2 + 2 + 5 sts from lower in row, turn. (19 sts)

Row 7: Ch1, [1dc in each of next 5 sts, dc2tog] 2 times, 1dc in each of next 5 sts, turn. (17 sts)

Row 8: Ch1, 1dc in each st, turn. (17 sts)

Row 9: Ch1, 1dc in each of next 4 sts, dc2tog, 1dc in each of next 5 sts, dc2tog, 1dc in each of next 4 sts, turn. (15 sts)

Row 10: Ch1, 1dc in each st, turn. (15 sts)

Row 11: Ch1, 1dc in each of next 2 sts, dc2tog, 1dc in each of next 7 sts, dc2tog, 1dc in each of next 2 sts, turn. (13 sts)

Row 12: Ch1, 1dc in each of next 13 sts, then ch4 for first arm, turn.

Row 13: Miss 1 ch, 1dc in next 3 ch, 1dc in next 13 body sts, ch4 for second arm, turn.

Row 14: Miss 1 ch, 1dc in next 3 ch, 1dc in each of 16 sts, turn. (19 sts)

Row 15: Ch1, 1dc in each of next 6 sts, dc2tog, 1dc in each of next 3 sts, dc2tog, 1dc in each of next 6 sts, turn. (17 sts)

Rows 16–17: Ch1, 1dc in each st, turn. (17 sts)

Row 18: Ch1, 1dc in each of next 5 sts, dc2tog, 1dc in each of next 3 sts, dc2tog, 1dc in each of next 5 sts, turn. (15 sts)

Row 19: Ch1, 1dc in each st, turn. (15 sts)
Row 20: Ch1, 1dc in each of next 12 sts, TWOFR. (12 sts)

Head
Row 1: Ch1, dc2tog, 1dc in each of next 5 sts, dc2tog, TWOFR. (7 sts)
Row 2: Ch1, 1dc in each st, turn. (7 sts)
Row 3: Ch1, [1dc in next st, 2dc in next st] 3 times, 1dc in next st, turn. (10 sts)
Row 4: Ch1, 1dc in each st, turn. (10 sts)
Row 5: Ch1, 2dc in each of next 2 sts, 1dc in next st, 2dc in each of next 4 sts, 1dc in next st, 2dc in each of next 2 sts, turn. (18 sts)
Row 6: Ch1, 1dc in each st, turn. (18 sts)
Row 7: Ch1, 1dc in each of next 2 sts, 2dc in next st, 1dc in each of next 3 sts, 2dc in next st, 1dc in each of next 4 sts, 2dc in next st, 1dc in each of next 2 sts, ch1, TWOFR, 1dc in each of next 11 sts, ch1, TWOFR, 1dc in each of next 9 sts, ch1, TWOFR, 1dc in each of next 7 sts, ch1, TWOFR, 1dc in each of next 5 sts, ch1, TWOFR, 1dc in each of next 3 sts, ch1, TWOFR, 1dc in each of next 3 sts, 1dc in each of 2 + 2 + 1 sts, 2dc in next st and 1dc in each of last 2 sts from lower in row, turn. (22 sts)
Row 8: Ch1, 1dc in each of 12 sts and 1dc in each of 2 + 2 + 6 sts from lower in row, turn. (22 sts)
Row 9: Ch1, 1dc in next st, 2dc in next st, 1dc in each of next 5 sts, [dc2tog] 4 times, 1dc in each of next 5 sts, 2dc in next st, 1dc in next st, turn. (20 sts)
Row 10: Ch1, 1dc in each st, turn. (20 sts)
Row 11: Ch1, 1dc in each of next 9 sts, dc2tog, 1dc in each of next 9 sts, turn. (19 sts)
Row 12: Ch1, 1dc in each st, turn. (19 sts)

Finishing

Weave in all ends. Sew granny square paws to end of arms with whip st. Sew front and back of bear together with whip st, stuffing as you go.
Embroider nose and eyes or attach safety toy eyes securely.

scarf

Starting Square

Using C and 4.0mm (US size G/6) hook, ch4, join with ss to form a ring.
Rnd 1: Ch2, 2htr in ring, *ch2, 3htr in ring; rep from * 2 times more, ch2, join with ss in top of first ch-2.
Fasten off C.
Rnd 2: Attach B in any corner sp, ch2, [2htr, ch2, 3htr] in same sp, *ch1, [3htr, ch2, 3htr] in next corner sp; rep from * 2 times more, ch1, join with ss in top of first ch-2.
Fasten off.

Make 7 more squares, using the join-as-you-go method (see page 121) on Rnd 2, to make a strip of 8 squares. Attach C in any st and work dc edging around entire strip, working 2dc in each of 2 ch in corner sps.
Fasten off.

Finishing

Weave in all ends. Attach button to centre of 2nd square from one end and use centre sp in second square from opposite end as buttonhole. Alternatively, scarf can be tied on.

Row 13: Ch1, 1dc in each of next 2 sts, dc2tog, 1dc in each of next 11 sts, dc2tog, 1dc in each of next 2 sts, turn. (17 sts)
Row 14: Ch1, 1dc in each st, turn. (17 sts)
Row 15: Ch1, dc2tog, 1dc in each of next 13 sts, ch1, TWOFR, 1dc in each of next 12 sts, ch1, TWOFR, 1dc in each of next 10 sts, ch1, TWOFR, 1dc in each of next 8 sts, ch1, TWOFR, 1dc in each of next 6 sts, ch1, TWOFR, 1dc in each of next 4 sts, ch1, TWOFR, 1dc in each of next 4 sts, 1dc in each of 2 + 2 + 2 sts and dc2tog over last 2 sts from lower in row, turn. (15 sts)
Row 16: Ch1, 1dc in each of 9 sts and 1dc in each of 2 + 2 + 2 sts from lower in row, turn. (15 sts)
Work ears as for Back of head.

chapter 4

useful information

This section contains instructions for all the basic crochet
techniques you will need, plus details of all the abbreviations and
special abbreviations used in the patterns. I've also
included a list of useful websites for yarns and
other materials.

Holding the hook

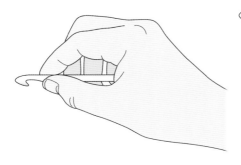

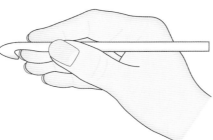

Hold the hook in the dominant hand either like a pencil, as shown above, or like a knife, as shown left. Both holds are correct so use whichever feels most comfortable.

Holding the yarn

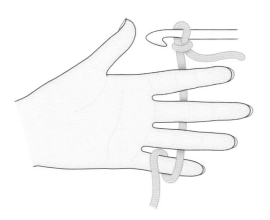

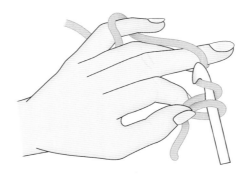

Lift the middle finger to tension the yarn and hold the work with the first finger and thumb, as illustrated above right.

Alternatively, lift the first finger to tension the yarn and hold the work with the middle finger and thumb.

On the non-dominant hand, wrap the yarn around the little finger, then across the back of the other fingers – or take it over the palm side of the ring finger, and back of middle and first finger, whichever feels most comfortable.

Making a chain (ch)

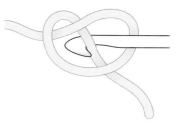

1. Start with a slip knot; make a loop in the yarn, insert the hook and catch the back strand.

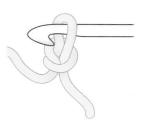

2. Pull the yarn through to make a loop, then gently pull on both ends to close the loop on the hook.

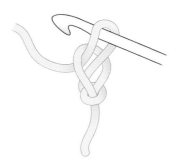

3. Hold the slip knot with the non-dominant hand and push the hook forward and under the tensioned yarn, catching the yarn, then pull the yarn through the loop on the hook. One chain made.

Useful Information   113

Yarn round hook (yrh)

Also known as yarn over (yo), or sometimes
yarn over hook (yoh). The hook should
always swing under the tensioned yarn,
toward the back.

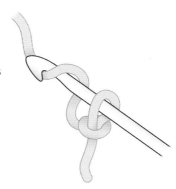

Chain ring/circle

If you are crocheting a round shape, one way of starting off is by crocheting a number
of chains following the instructions in your pattern, and then joining them into a ring.

1. To join the chain into a ring, insert the
crochet hook into the first chain made
(not into the slip knot), yarn round hook,
then pull the yarn through the chain and
through the loop on your hook at the
same time, creating a slip stitch and
forming a ring.

2. You will now have a ring
ready to work into according
to your pattern.

Slip stitch (ss)

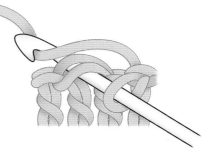

Insert the hook into the stitch or
chain required, yarn round hook
and pull through both work AND
loop on hook without taking the
yarn round the hook again. One
slip stitch made.

Double crochet (dc)

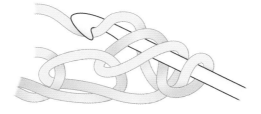

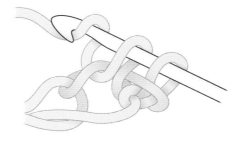

1. Insert the hook into the stitch or chain required. Yarn round hook and pull up a loop (2 loops on hook).

2. Yarn round hook again and pull through both loops on the hook. One double crochet made.

Half treble (htr)

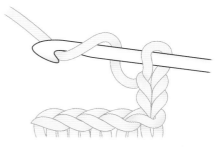

1. Yarn round hook first, then insert the hook into the stitch or chain required.

2. Yarn round hook and pull up a loop (3 loops on hook).

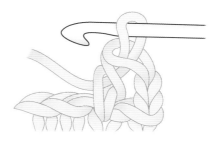

3. Yarn round hook and pull through all three loops on the hook. One half-treble made.

Treble (tr)

1. Yarn round hook first, then insert the hook into the stitch or chain required. Yarn round hook and pull up a loop (3 loops on hook).

2. Yarn round hook and pull through two loops on the hook (2 loops on hook).

3. Yarn round hook, pull through the last two loops on the hook. One treble made.

Double treble (dtr)

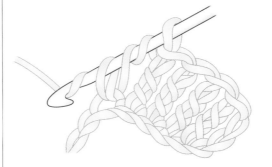

Yarn round hook twice first, then insert the hook into the stitch or chain required. Yarn round hook and pull up a loop, yarn round hook and pull through two loops, yarn round hook and pull through two loops again, yarn round hook and pull through the last two loops on the hook. One double treble made.

Double crochet 2 together (dc2tog)

1. Insert the hook into the next stitch, yarn round hook, pull up a loop, then insert the hook into the next stitch.

2. Yarn round hook and pull up a loop, yarn round hook and pull through all three loops on the hook. One double crochet 2 together decrease made.

Fastening (finishing) off crochet

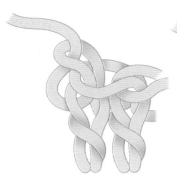

2. Pull the tail all the way through the remaining loop on the hook to secure the end.

1. Cut the yarn, leaving a minimum 10cm (4in) tail – leave a longer tail for projects requiring a long end for sewing.

Chain space (ch sp)

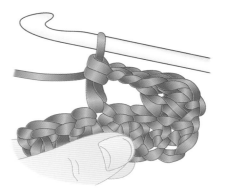

1. A chain space is the space that has been made under a chain in the previous round or row and falls in between other stitches.

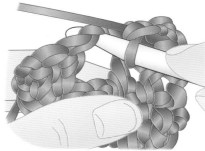

2. Stitches into a chain space are made directly into the hole created under the chain and not into the chain stitches themselves.

Half treble 2 together (htr2tog)

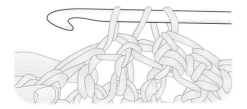 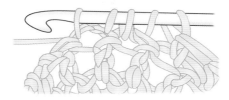 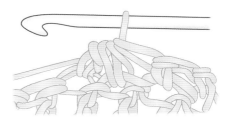

1. Yarn round hook, insert the hook into the next stitch, yarn round hook and pull up a loop.

2. Yarn round hook, insert the hook into the next stitch, yarn round hook and pull up a loop (5 loops on hook).

3. Yarn round hook and pull through all five loops on the hook. One half treble 2 together decrease made. Treble 2 together (tr2tog), is worked using the same basic technique.

Working in continuous spiral rounds

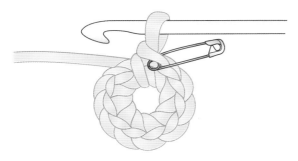

A chain is not necessary at the beginning of the round, or a slip stitch at the end. Start a new round in the first stitch of the previous round. Use a stitch marker to mark the first stitch of the round.

No. of chain needed for each st when working rounds or rows:

Double crochet = 1 chain
Half treble = 2 chain
Treble = 3 chain
Double treble = 4 chain

Working in rounds

Each round is begun with the number of chain required to create the height you need for the stitch you are working (see below left). At the end of the round, the last stitch is joined to the first with a slip stitch.

Working in rows

When working in straight rows, make a turning chain at the end to create the height you need for the stitch you are working with (see far left for number of chain required). Remember to crochet into the turning chain at the end of the following row.

Around the post stitch

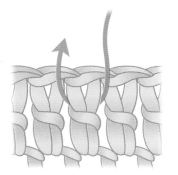

Front post stitch

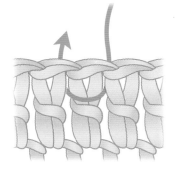

Back post stitch

Instead of inserting the hook into the V of the required stitch, insert it around the vertical part (the post) of the stitch from the row below.

Double crochet join

Insert the hook through both stitches to be joined, yarn round hook and pull up a loop, yarn round hook and pull through both loops on the hook.

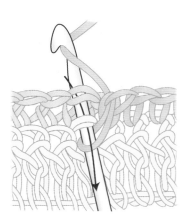

Join-as-you-go method

Finish one square completely following the instructions in the pattern – this will be the 'starting square' in the following steps.
Work the next square until you reach the last round – this square is referred to as the 'current square' in the following steps.

1. Work the first side of the current square including the first corner grouping (first set of 3htr or 3tr), then instead of making ch2 for the corner sp, insert the hook into the corner sp of the starting square from underneath as shown.

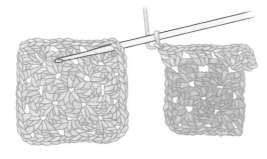

2. 1dc into the corner sp of the starting square (counts as first of 2-ch for the corner sp), ch1, then work the second 3htr or 3tr grouping into the corner sp of the current square as usual.

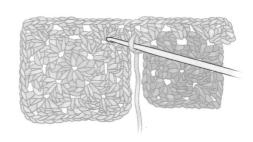

3. To continue joining the squares together, instead of ch1, work 1dc into the next side sp of the starting square.

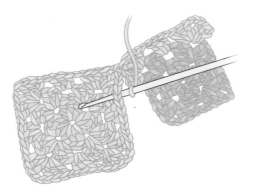

4. Work 3htr or 3tr in the next side sp of the current square. Continue replacing each ch-1 at the sides of the current square with 1dc into the next side sp of the starting square, and replacing the first of the ch-2 at the corner sp of the current square with 1dc into the corner sp of the starting square.

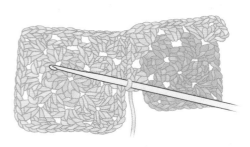

5. When the current square is joined to the starting square along one side, continue around and finish the final round of the current square as normal.

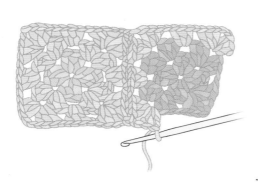

6. When joining a current square to two previous squares, replace both corner ch of the current square with 1dc into each adjoining square.

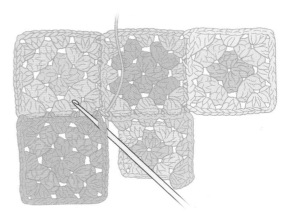

abbreviations

alt:	alternate/alternating
beg:	beginning
bphtr:	work htr around back post of stitch
CC:	contrast colour
ch:	chain
cont:	continue
dc:	double crochet
dc2tog:	double crochet 2 sts together
dtr:	double treble
fphtr:	work htr around front post of stitch
htr:	half treble
htr2tog:	half treble 2 sts together
inc:	including
MC:	main colour
prev:	previous
rem:	remaining
rep:	repeat
Rnd:	round
RS:	right side
sp:	space
ss:	slip stitch
st(s):	stitch(es)
tr:	treble
WS:	wrong side
yrh:	yarn round hook

Special abbreviations

2-tr cluster: two-treble cluster – [yrh, insert into sp/st/ch, yrh, pull through a loop, yrh, pull through 2 loops] 2 times, yrh, pull through all 3 loops on hook.

3-tr cluster: three-treble cluster – [yrh, insert into sp/st/ch, yrh, pull through a loop, yrh, pull through 2 loops] 3 times, yrh, pull through all 4 loops on hook.

5-dtr cluster: five-double treble cluster – *yrh 2 times, insert into sp/st/ch, yrh, pull through a loop, [yrh, pull through 2 loops] 2 times; rep from * 4 times more, yrh, pull through all 6 loops on hook.

6-dtr cluster: six-double treble cluster – *yrh 2 times, insert into sp/st/ch, yrh, pull through a loop, [yrh, pull through 2 loops] 2 times; rep from * 5 times more, yrh, pull through all 7 loops on hook.

BPSS: back post slip stitch – insert hook from back to front to back around post of st, yrh, pull through post of st and loop on hook without taking yrh again.

TWFR: turn without finishing row – stop at this point without finishing the row, turn the work and begin working back along the row.

useful websites

DMC
www.dmc.com

Coats Crafts
www.coatscrafts.co.uk

Designer Yarns
www.designeryarns.uk.com

Rowan Yarns
www.knitrowan.com

Debbie Bliss
www.debbieblissonline.com

Crafty Yarn
www.crafty-yarn.co.uk

Black Sheep Wools
www.blacksheepwools.com

Yarnstick
www.yarnstick.co.uk

Purplelinda Crafts
www.purplelindacrafts.co.uk

Catherine Hirst
www.catherinehirst.com

acknowledgements

I am very grateful to all those who helped make this book possible. Gillian Haslam at Cico Books was, as always, patient, kind and encouraging. My editor, Marie Clayton, is simply brilliant and I'd also like to thank Susan Horan for her meticulous pattern checking. The gorgeous photographs by Emma Mitchell and fantastic styling by Sophie Martell showcased the projects beautifully, and Roger Hammond's great page design brought everything together.

I have to thank my mother-in-law Evelyn and good friend Emma for putting in many hours on the bedcover while I got on with other projects – you ladies saved my bacon! Big, furry smooches go to the fabulous Elvis who modelled the dog coat, as well as her lovely owner Kate.

Finally, nothing in my life would ever go quite so well if it weren't for the support and encouragement of my wonderful husband Julian; lots of love from your madly-crocheting wife!